Play Drums Today!

A Complete Guide to the Basics

PLAYBACK+
Speed • Pitch • Balance • Loop

To access audio and video visit:
www.halleonard.com/mylibrary

Enter Code
2328-5805-3945-4418

by Scott Schroedl

Recording Credits:
Todd Greene, Producer
Jake Johnson, Engineer
Doug Boduch, Guitar
Scott Schroedl, Drums
Tom McGirr, Bass
Warren Wiegratz, Keyboards
Andy Drefs, Narration

ISBN 978-1-5400-5236-0

Visit Hal Leonard Online at
www.halleonard.com

Contact us:
Hal Leonard
7777 West Bluemound Road
Milwaukee, WI 53213
Email: info@halleonard.com

In Europe, contact:
Hal Leonard Europe Limited
42 Wigmore Street
Marylebone, London, W1U 2RN
Email: info@halleonardeurope.com

In Australia, contact:
Hal Leonard Australia Pty. Ltd.
4 Lentara Court
Cheltenham, Victoria, 3192 Australia
Email: info@halleonard.com.au

Introduction

Track 1

Welcome to *Play Drums Today!*—the series designed to get you playing any style of music, from rock to blues to country to jazz. Whatever your tastes, *Play Drums Today!* will give you the start you need.

About the Audio & Video

It's easy and fun to play drums, and the accompanying audio will make your learning even more enjoyable, as we take you step by step through each lesson and play many of the examples with a full band. Much like with real lessons, the best way to learn the material is to read and practice awhile first on your own, then listen to the audio. With *Play Drums Today!*, you can learn at your own pace. If there is ever something that you don't quite understand the first time through, go back to the audio and listen again. Every musical track has been given a track number, so if you want to practice a song again, you can find it right away.

Some lessons in the book include video, so you can see and hear the material being taught. Audio and videos are indicated with icons.

Audio Icon   Video Icon

Contents

The Basics

Setting Up Your Drums

Take a look at the drumset below and the names associated with each piece. This is considered a basic five-piece drumset. You may have more tom-toms, another bass drum, or even more cymbals, but this is where it all begins. Notice the position of the drums and cymbals, and arrange yours in a similar layout.

Ride cymbal　　　　Tom-toms　　　　Crash cymbal

Hi-hat

Snare drum

Floor tom　　　　Bass drum

Parts of Your Instrument

All parts of the sticks, drums, and cymbals are used when playing. Take a minute to learn the parts of each, so you'll know exactly what we're talking about later.

Stick

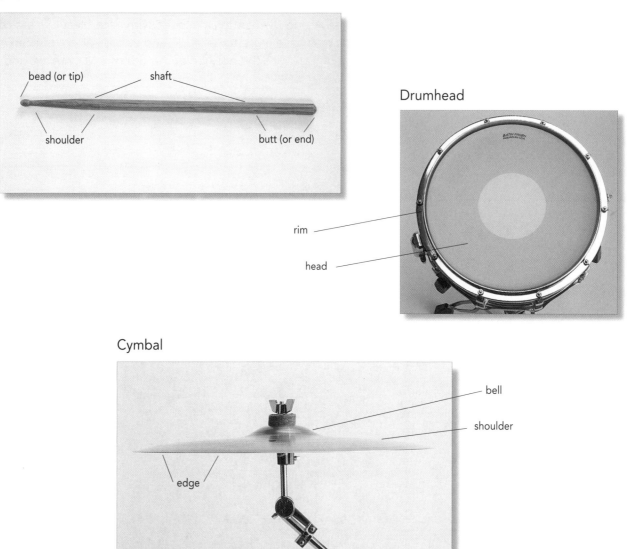

Drumhead

Cymbal

Getting Started

Let's begin by adjusting your stool. Make sure it isn't too high or too low. Set your stool height so that, when you're sitting, your legs are bent at 90 degrees. You may decide later to sit slightly higher as you get comfortable with your set.

Now straddle the snare drum. Place your right foot on the bass drum pedal and your left foot on the hi-hat pedal.

How to Hold Your Sticks

Drumsticks come in many different sizes to fit varying hand sizes and playing styles. Larger sticks are able to produce more volume with less effort; smaller sticks make it easier to keep the volume under control. There are two basic ways to hold your sticks: matched grip and traditional grip.

matched grip   traditional grip

Between the two grips, only the left hand is different. Matched grip is easier to learn since the technique for both hands is the same. Try both, and decide what works better for you.

matched grip
(both hands)

traditional grip
(left hand)

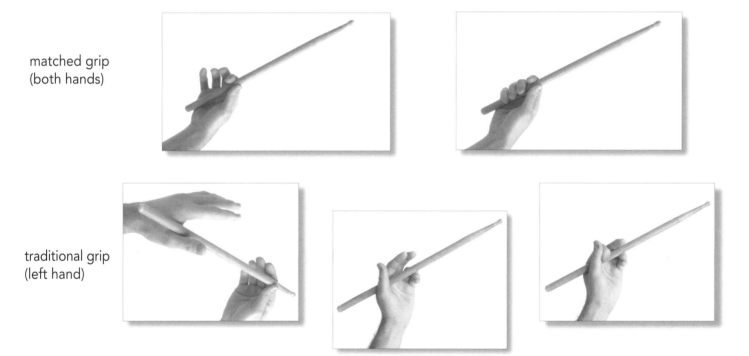

Got a Metronome?

As a drummer, your most important job is to keep a steady, accurate, and appropriate **tempo**. Tempo means the "speed" at which the music is played.

A **metronome** is a device that keeps perfect time. You simply dial up the number of beats per minute, and the metronome begins clicking the beat. The best type of metronome for drummers is digital with an earphone jack (preferably with a volume control) so you can wear headphones to hear the "click" when practicing your drums.

On the accompanying audio, you'll hear a metronome play "clicks" before each musical example to give you the appropriate tempo.

How to Read Music

Music is written with notes and rests. A **note** means to "play"; a **rest** means to "rest" (or "pause").

Staff & Clef

All notes or rests are written on a **staff**, which consists of five lines and four spaces. For drummers, each line and space represents a different piece of your drumset.

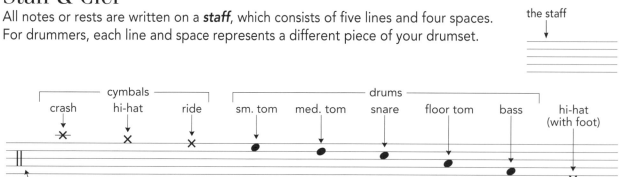

Pitched instruments (such as guitars and keyboards) also use a staff, but the lines and spaces represent different musical tones. A symbol called a **percussion clef** tells you that this is a staff for drums.

Rhythm

Every note or rest has a rhythmic value. This determines how long, or for how many beats, it will last

To help you keep track of the beats in a song, notes on a staff are divided into **measures**, or "bars."

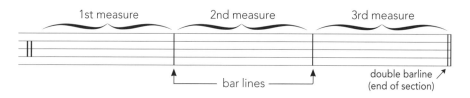

A **time signature** appears at the beginning of a song to indicate how many beats will appear in each measure. It contains two numbers: The top number tells you how many beats will be in each measure; the bottom number tells you what type of note will equal one beat.

Any combination of notes or rests can appear in a measure, but they must always add up to the number of beats indicated in the time signature. To keep track of the beats, it helps to count as you play:

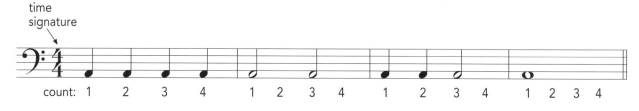

The Ride Cymbal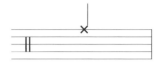

Track 2

The first instrument we'll learn on the drumset is the *ride cymbal*. This is usually the largest cymbal, located on your right side. It's called the ride cymbal because you "ride" on it—that is, you maintain a steady pattern.

■ Ride cymbal is written on the top line of the staff, stems up.

How to Play It

The ride cymbal can be played several different ways to produce different sounds. The most common way is to play with the bead (or tip) of the stick on the shoulder of the cymbal about two-thirds in from the outer edge.

Another sound is produced by playing the bead of the stick on the bell (the raised middle) of the ride cymbal.

To produce a heavier cutting sound, try playing the shoulder of the stick on the bell.

Note: You may use any of the three ways to play the ride. They are not usually notated differently, so use your ear to decide what sounds best for the style of music you are playing.

Let's begin by playing quarter notes on the ride cymbal. Count out loud "1, 2, 3, 4" as you play the following notes with the right hand.

Track 3

Quarter Ride #1

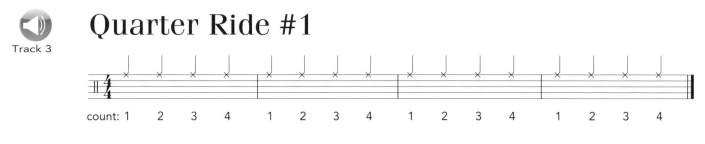

count: 1   2   3   4   1   2   3   4   1   2   3   4   1   2   3   4

The next example uses quarter notes and quarter rests. Keep counting even though you aren't playing during the rests.

Track 4

Quarter Ride #2

count: 1   2   3   4   1   2   3   4   1   2   3   4   1   2   3   4

You may notice that the ride cymbal keeps ringing during a rest. Don't worry; that's just the cymbal's natural sustain. Concentrate on playing on the correct beats and *not* playing during rests.

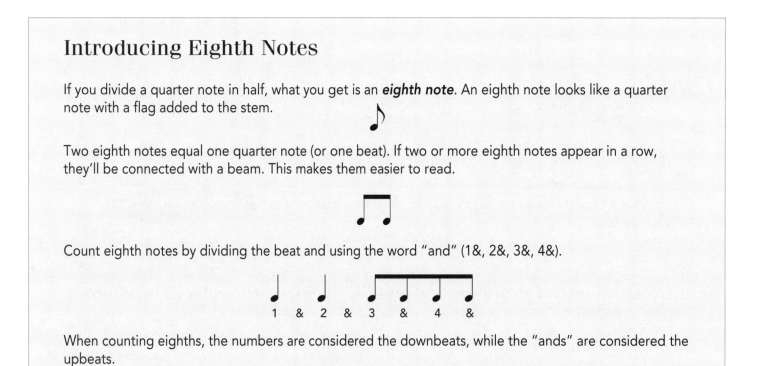

Introducing Eighth Notes

If you divide a quarter note in half, what you get is an **eighth note**. An eighth note looks like a quarter note with a flag added to the stem.

Two eighth notes equal one quarter note (or one beat). If two or more eighth notes appear in a row, they'll be connected with a beam. This makes them easier to read.

Count eighth notes by dividing the beat and using the word "and" (1&, 2&, 3&, 4&).

1 & 2 & 3 & 4 &

When counting eighths, the numbers are considered the downbeats, while the "ands" are considered the upbeats.

Now try playing eighth notes on the ride. Don't forget to count along. Eighth notes are played twice as fast as quarter notes.

Track 5

Eighth-Note Ride

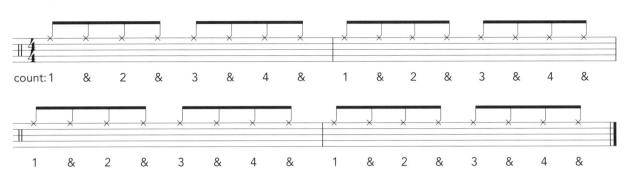

We'll combine quarter notes and eighth notes in the next example. It may be helpful to count "and" between the quarter notes to better understand how quarters and eighths fit together.

Track 6

Combining Quarters & Eighths

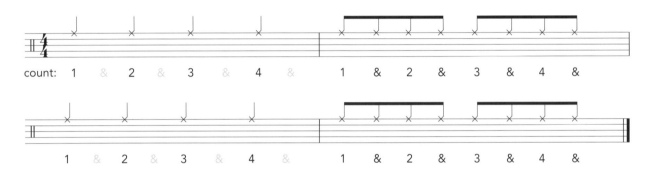

Mixing It Up

Track 7

► Keep counting aloud (or silently) as you play.

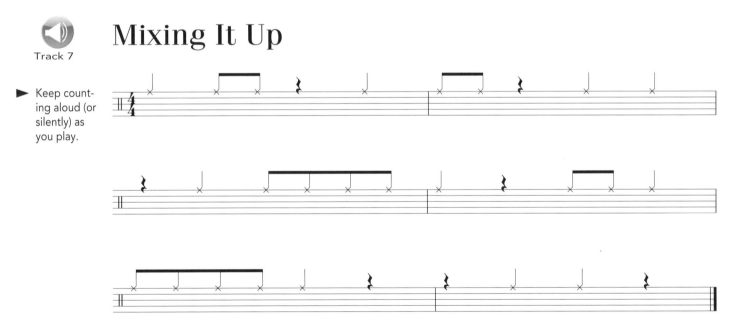

The Snare Drum

Track 8

When seated behind your drums with your feet on the pedals, the *snare* is the drum between your legs. This is one of the most important drums in the set. It's used to provide the *backbeat* (beats 2 and 4) in popular songs—as well as other flashy things we'll talk about later.

■ Snare drum is written on the third space of the staff from the bottom.

Take a moment now to adjust the height of your snare drum. You may want to tilt it slightly towards you. It should be high enough that you don't hit your legs when playing it.

How to Play It

When hitting the snare drum, don't press the stick into the head (which produces a buzzing sound), but rather let it bounce back naturally. Play in the center of the drum as in the following photo.

What makes the snare drum different from the other drums are the metal strands (or "snares") touching the bottom head. You can turn these off by flipping the throw-off lever on the side of the drum, which releases the snares and prevents them from vibrating against the head.

To get an idea of how the snare drum typically is used in a groove, try the next examples with the stick in your left hand, playing some popular backbeat patterns.

Track 9

Backbeats #1

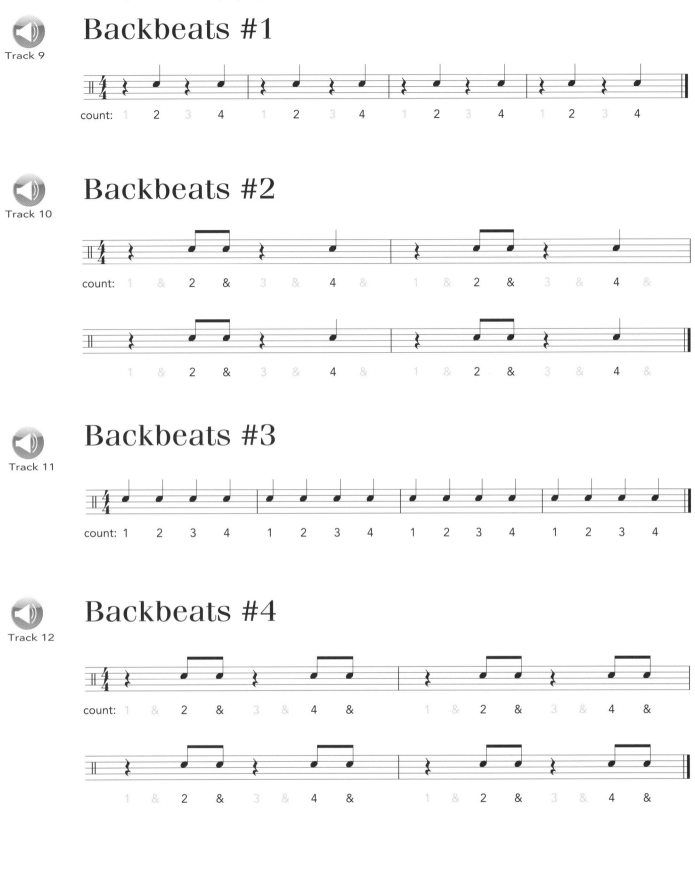

Track 10

Backbeats #2

Track 11

Backbeats #3

Track 12

Backbeats #4

Try playing the ride cymbal and snare drum together for the next examples. Keep in mind, the notes that are vertically in line will be played together at the same time.

Track 13

Quarter Ride/Snare

Track 14

Eighth Ride/Snare

► It may help to start with the ride cymbal first, and then add the snare.

Track 15

Hands Together

Track 16

Two And/Four And

The Bass Drum

Track 17

The function of the **bass drum** is to provide the "boom" and "drive" to the grooves.

■ Bass drum is written on the lowest space of the staff with the stem down.

How to Play It

Bass drum is played by pushing down the pedal with your right foot. Sit close enough so that you are pushing the pedal down, not forward.

There are two ways of playing the bass drum. One way is to play with your foot flat on the pedal, using just your ankle to propel the beater into the head. Another option is to play with your heel up. When playing this way, you'll use your whole leg to move the pedal, pivoting from the hip. Many rock drummers prefer the "heel up" approach to get more volume out of the drum. Some use both techniques depending on the style of music they're playing. Try both, and decide which works best for you.

Foot flat

Heel up

Playin' the Bass

Track 18

► Don't forget to count as you play.

Now that you have a feel for playing the bass drum, try the next examples combining it with the other parts of the drumset you already know.

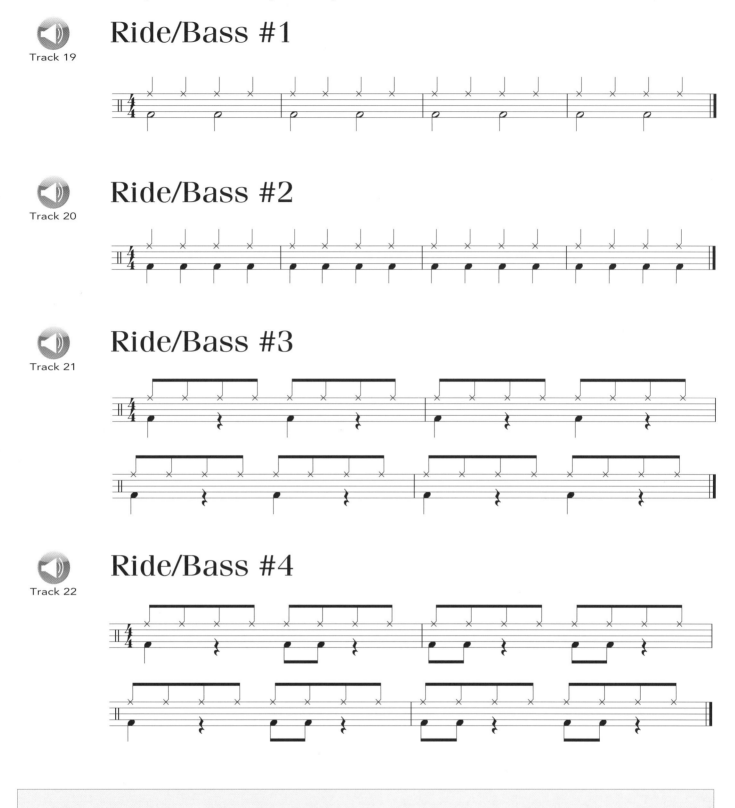

Ride/Bass #1

Track 19

Ride/Bass #2

Track 20

Ride/Bass #3

Track 21

Ride/Bass #4

Track 22

How to Play It, Part 2

Another thing to consider when playing the bass drum is how the beater strikes the drumhead. When you strike the drum, you can hold the beater into the head until just before playing the next note. This is called "burying the beater." Or, for a more open sound, try hitting the drumhead and bringing the beater back immediately. Many jazz players prefer this more natural sound. Again, decide which sounds best to you and your musical situation.

Bass/Snare Beats

Track 23

Here are a few basic rock beats to play along with the band. Remember to practice slowly, and gradually speed up your tempos as you feel more confident.

Basic Beat

Track 24

► Start with the ride, then add bass and snare.

Four on the Floor

Track 25

Surfin'

Track 26

Pop Beat

Track 27

The Hi-Hat

Track 28

The **hi-hat** cymbals are another important part of the drumset. They're used as an alternative to the ride cymbal and can be played several different ways: closed, open, half-open (sloshy) with the sticks, or closed with the foot.

When playing the hi-hat, you can hit the cymbals on the edge with the shoulder of the stick or on the shoulder of the top cymbal with the bead of the stick to create different sounds.

Closed Hi-Hat

With your left foot on the hi-hat pedal holding the cymbals closed tightly, strike the hi-hat with your right stick.

■ Closed hi-hat is written on the top space above the staff.

Track 29

Closed Hat

Adjusting Your Hi-Hat

Hi-hat is typically played by the right hand, while the left hand plays the snare underneath. This means that the two hands cross over each other when playing. The first thing you'll want to do then is set up your hi-hat cymbals high enough on the stand that when you cross over with your right hand to play them, your left hand won't interfere. You can adjust the height of both cymbals by loosening the wing screw located midway along the stand.

Once that's done, raise the top cymbal about an inch above the bottom cymbal, and tighten it with the other wing screw (the one *above* the hi-hat cymbals). Now look under the bottom cymbal for the tilting mechanism. Turn this screw in to angle the bottom cymbal—so that when you step on the pedal, you don't create an air pocket between the cymbals. (This becomes important when you start playing open and closed hi-hat with the foot.)

wing screw

tilt screw

Half-Open (Sloshy) Hi-Hat

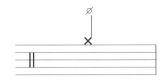

Half-open (sloshy) hi-hat notes is written on the top space above the staff, but has an "o" with a line through it above each note.

To achieve the half-open "sloshy" sound, release some pressure on the pedal so that, when you hit the cymbals, you hear a "sizzle." You can also think of this as sort of "sloppy" closed hat sound.

Sloshy Hat

Track 30

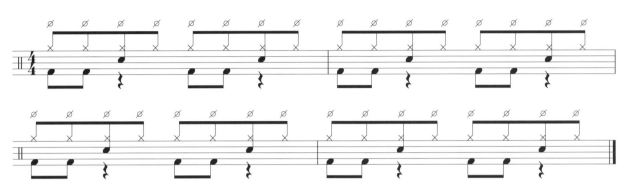

Foot Hi-Hat

You can also play the hi-hats without hitting them—by stepping on the pedal with your left foot.

■ Hi-hat played with the foot is written just below the staff, stem down.

Starting position for this technique is with your foot on the pedal, holding the cymbals closed. Just before the note to be played, open the cymbals by lifting your foot. Close the cymbals on the beat to be played, and hold them closed until you need to play them again. This way, you're not holding the cymbals open waiting for the next note. It's also easier to keep your balance on the stool.

For the next exercises, use your right hand on the ride cymbal and your left foot on the hi-hat pedal.

Track 31

Foot Hat Practice

The One-Measure Repeat Sign

The symbol (✗) means to repeat the previous measure.

Now try adding the snare and bass drum to test your four-way coordination.

Track 32

Coordination

This example uses quarter notes with your hi-hat foot and eighth notes on the ride cymbal.

Track 33

Quarter Foot Hat

► Start with the ride, then add the foot hi-hat.

Once again, add the bass and snare to the pattern. If you find it difficult playing all of the parts together, try breaking them down into three parts and add the fourth once you get going. For example, play the ride, bass, and snare parts together, and add the hi-hat with the foot once you're comfortable.

Track 34

Practice Makes Perfect

Open Hi-Hat

Using the open hi-hat occasionally will add color and punctuation to a beat.

■ Open hi-hat looks just like closed hi-hat, but with an "o" (for "open") above it.

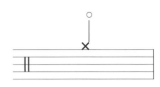

When executing the open hi-hat, begin lifting your left foot (on the hi-hat pedal) just before you hit the cymbals with the stick. You don't want to hit the cymbals after they are completely open, but rather as they are opening—so the two cymbals hit together to produce a sizzle sound on the way open.

Track 35

Executing the Open Hi-Hat

► Open hi-hat is usually followed by closed hi-hat with the foot.

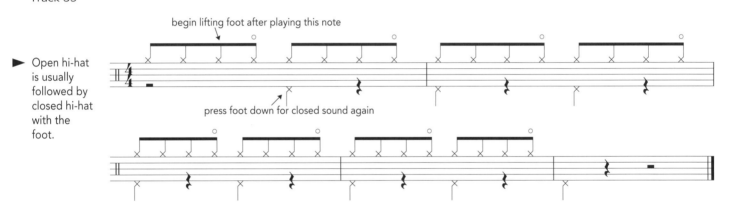

Now incorporate this into the next groove.

Track 36

Open/Closed Hats

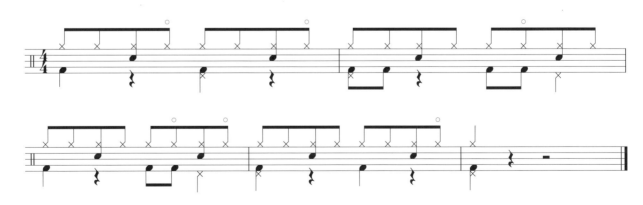

Independence and Coordination

The following exercises will increase independence and coordination between your hands and feet. If these are a challenge for you—and they should be—take them *slow*. You'll naturally increase your speed when you're ready.

We begin with quarter notes on the ride cymbal and quarter and eighth notes on the bass drum.

Between the Quarters

Track 37

► Start with the ride, then add the bass drum.

Introducing the Eighth Rest

Eighth rests (♪) have the same value as eighth notes, but you pause instead of playing.

To help you understand the eighth rest better, the next example will use an eighth-note ride. Line up the bass drum notes with the steady eighth ride pattern. Notice where the eighth rests fall in the measure.

Eighth Resting

Track 38

Try the next hand coordination exercises.

Hand Coordinating #1

Track 39

Notice that in the next example, even though some of the ride notes are eighths because they are connected to the snare notes, the ride is still only playing beats 1, 2, 3, and 4.

Track 40

Hand Coordinating #2

Now add the snare, bass, and hi-hat together. Again, take it slow.

Track 41

Getting Groovy

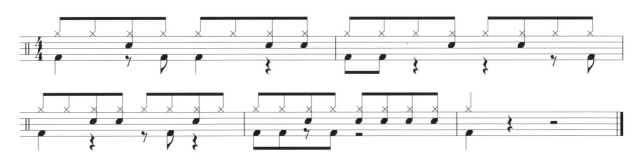

Track 42

More Groovy

Build It Up or Break It Down

If you have trouble coordinating parts in a groove, try either building the groove up or breaking it down:

Build It Up. Start with one element—like hi-hat. Then add another—like bass drum. Finally, add the last element—like the snare.

Break It Down. Try different combinations—like hi-hat and bass drum, hi-hat and snare, or bass drum and snare.

Putting It All Together

It's time for a review (and to have some fun!) using everything you've learned so far. Here are some one-bar grooves you can find in many popular songs today. These are not designed to be played one right after another, but on the audio you'll hear each one played twice, then one measure of "clicks," and then the next groove. On your own, practice each one over and over, repeating it until it sounds smooth. Also, try them at different tempos.

Track 43

► If these are difficult for you, break them down as you learned on page 21.

Ride Grooves

Closed Hi-Hat Grooves

Half-Open Hi-Hat Grooves

Open Hi-Hat Grooves

Repeat signs have two dots before or after a double bar line (||: :||). They simply tell you to repeat everything in between. If only one sign appears (:||), repeat from the beginning of the piece.

The Crash Cymbal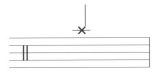

Track 44

The *crash cymbal* is used to accent changes in the music and mark different sections of a song. You may have only one crash cymbal on your set or many crashes, varying in size and thickness to produce different sounds.

■ Crash cymbal is written on a line just above the staff called a *ledger line*.

Try hitting the crash cymbal using your right stick. The cymbal should be struck on the edge with the shoulder of the stick hitting a glancing blow. Later on, you may want to also try hitting crashes with your left stick, but for right now, use your right.

In the next example, we'll start off using quarter-note crashes to give you more time to get to the ride cymbal. Notice that the crash on beat 4 of the second measure is followed by another crash on beat 1 of the next measure. Keep your stick by the crash to play these two in a row, rather than moving it back toward the ride.

Crashing

Track 45

Now we'll use eighth notes following the crash cymbal. Be sure to get to the ride fast enough, concentrating on making a smooth transition.

Crash 'n' Ride

Track 46

As mentioned before, the crash cymbal is often used to mark changes in the music. Here, the crash appears every four measures, coinciding with a switch from the ride cymbal to the half-open hi-hat. You may want to focus on these transitions to get comfortable moving between cymbals.

Track 47

Moving Between Cymbals

Four-Bar Phrases—Beats & Fills

Notice how the groove above changes every four measures (almost like a mini-song)? This is common in music. In fact, drum music often follows a four-bar formula that goes something like this…

Beat

A basic groove that lasts three measures or so.

Fill

A short break in the groove—a lick that "fills in the gaps" of the music and/or signals the end of a phrase. It's kind of like a mini-solo.

Cymbal crash

The icing on the cake. The crash brings the fill to a climax and signals the start of the next phrase or section.

Keep your eyes and ears open; we'll see a lot more four-bar phrases—and learn a lot more beats and fills—as we go on.

More Rhythms

Track 48

We've learned half notes, quarter notes, eighth notes, and their respective rests. Now it's time to look at some new rhythms.

Sixteenth Notes

Let's start with *sixteenth notes*. These look like eighth notes but with a second flag added to the stem.

Two or more sixteenth notes are joined together with two beams.

Basically, if you divide an eighth note in half, what you get is a sixteenth note. Two sixteenth notes equal one eighth note; four sixteenth notes equal one quarter note. Here's a diagram showing the relationship of sixteenth notes to all the rhythmic values you've learned.

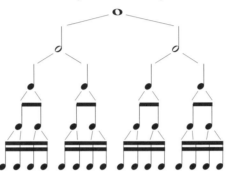

Sixteenth rests have the same value as the sixteenth notes, but are silent. Sixteenth rests look like an eighth rest on top of another eighth rest:

To count sixteenth notes (and sixteenth rests), say "1 e & a, 2 e & a, 3 e & a, 4 e & a."

$$1 \ e \ \& \ a \quad 2 \ e \ \& \ a \quad 3 \ e \ \& \ a \quad 4 \ e \ \& \ a$$

Play the next example alternating between your right and left hands using sixteenth notes on the snare drum. Practice counting aloud to better understand the notes. Notice the bass drum is playing quarter notes on beats 1, 2, 3, and 4.

Sixteenth Study

Track 49

count: 1 e & a 2 e & a 3 e & a 4 e & a   1 e & a 2 e & a 3 e & a 4 e & a

In the next example, the sixteenth notes are on the ride cymbal. Play slowly at first, counting aloud.

Riding Along

Track 50

▶ Play the ride with your right stick and the snare with your left.

Track 51

The Hi-Hat: Alternating Hands

Here's a fun technique: Try moving both hands to the hi-hat. Play even sixteenths using the alternate sticking indicated (RLRL), but let your right hand move to the snare on beats 2 and 4. Be sure to get back to the hi-hat to keep the even sixteenth notes flowing!

Dotted Quarter and Eighth Notes

A *dot* extends a note or rest by one-half of its value. For drummers, the two most common are the dotted quarter and dotted eighth.

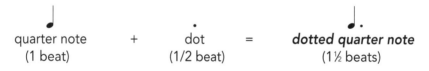

quarter note   +   dot   =   ***dotted quarter note***
(1 beat)   (1/2 beat)   (1½ beats)

NOTE: A dotted quarter is usually followed by an eighth note.

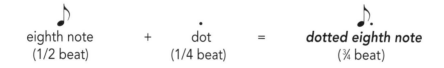

eighth note   +   dot   =   ***dotted eighth note***
(1/2 beat)   (1/4 beat)   (¾ beat)

NOTE: A dotted eighth is usually connected to a sixteenth, like this:

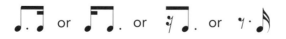

This next example uses dotted quarters on the bass drum. You may notice that, in playing terms, a dotted quarter note is not much different from a quarter note plus an eighth rest. (Since the bass drum doesn't actually sustain, either way sounds the same.)

Track 52

Dotted Quarter Kick

The next example uses dotted eighth notes combined with sixteenths on the bass drum. Notice the dotted eighth note and the dotted eighth rest are equal in value.

Track 53

Slow Groove

▶ Play the hi-hat with your right stick and the snare with your left.

Here are more one-bar grooves using dotted notes. Start slowly with these.

Track 54

Beats Galore

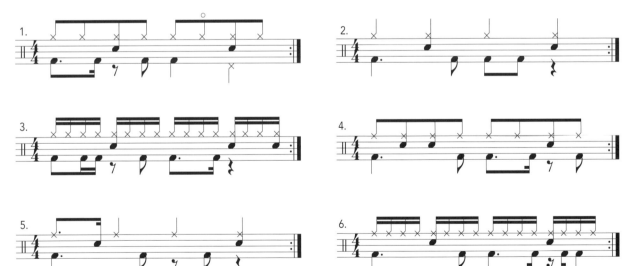

The Tom-Toms

Track 55

Now that we have the basics down, it's time to spice things up with the **tom-toms** (or "toms"). If you own a five-piece drumset, you should have three toms of different sizes. You may have more or less; it really doesn't matter. Toms are used to add tonal "color" to your sound.

Rack toms are mounted on the bass drum. When seated behind the drumset, the **small tom** should be on your left and the **medium tom** on the right. Adjust the angle of the rack toms so they are comfortable for you to reach and play. If they're angled too much, you may dent the drumheads easily. Conversely, if the drums are too flat, you'll hit the rims.

■ The small tom is written on the top space; the medium tom is written on the fourth line.

The **floor tom** is the largest drum besides the bass drum, and it has three legs, which allows it to be freestanding. Place the floor tom to the right of your right leg when your foot is on the bass drum pedal.

■ Floor tom is written on the space above the bass drum.

Toms are arranged in order of size, starting with the smallest on the left when you are seated behind your drums. Now that all your toms are adjusted properly, try hitting them to get comfortable with the reach. The toms should sound high to low from left to right.

Sticking With It

One of the most important things to notice when reading the following tom exercises is the right and left hand *sticking* (e.g., RLRL). Always follow the sticking indicated. This helps to avoid hand crossover and will get you playing these exercises faster and more smoothly.

Track 56

Around the Toms

Toms are great for use in fills. Practice each of these one-bar fills until smooth. On the track, you will hear each fill followed by one measure of "clicks" and then the next fill. (In the real world, this isn't how you'd normally play them, but it's good practice.)

Track 57

Tom Fills

▶ These will take practice. Be patient, and take them slowly at first.

Of course, you don't have to reserve the toms just for fills; you can also incorporate them into your beats.

Track 58

Tom Beat #1

Track 59

Tom Beat #2

For a real driving beat, play your right hand on the floor tom instead of the hi-hat or ride.

Track 60

Floor Tom Power

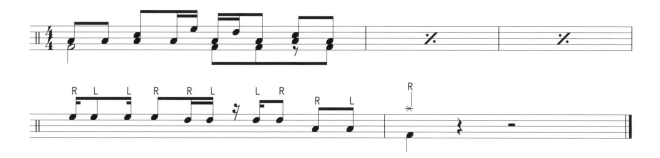

Special Techniques

Track 61

In this section, we'll introduce some of the finer points in drumset playing. Let's begin with accents.

Accents

An *accent* look like this: > Accents are placed above or beneath a note and tell you to play that note a little louder than the surrounding notes. This makes playing even the same rhythm sound different.

Try this example on the snare. Start with your right hand and alternate. Above the accents, we'll mark the hand you should be playing the accents with. Practice this slowly until you can play it as fast as on the track.

Track 62

Accenting Along

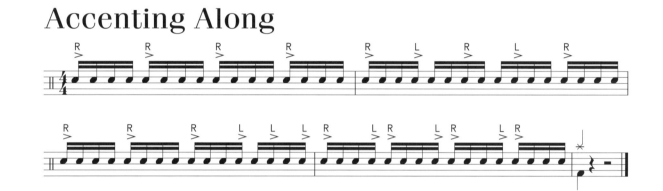

Now try some tom fills using accents.

Track 63

Diggin' In

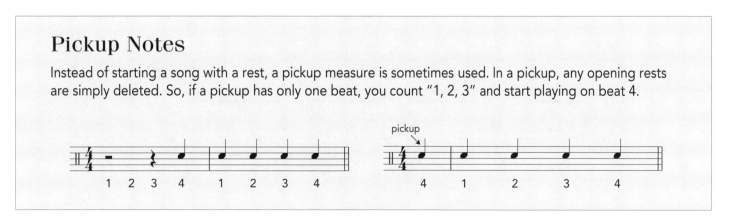

Pickup Notes

Instead of starting a song with a rest, a pickup measure is sometimes used. In a pickup, any opening rests are simply deleted. So, if a pickup has only one beat, you count "1, 2, 3" and start playing on beat 4.

For the next example, you will hear only three "clicks" and you will start on the "and" of beat 3.

Pick 'Em Up

Cross-Stick

The **cross-stick** (sometimes referred to as "rim click" or "side stick") sound is used quite frequently in ballads, and is popular in many other styles as well. To produce the cross-stick sound, flip the stick in your left hand around so that you are holding the shoulder of the stick. Lay the stick across the snare, as in the photo below, with the bead of the stick on the head, and the shaft closest to the butt end on the rim.

■ A circle around the snare drum indicates the cross-stick sound.

Crossing the Line

► Notice the open hi-hat in the second measure.

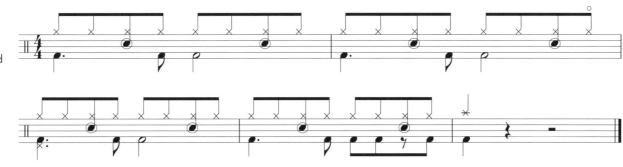

Half-Time Beat

Rim Shot

The *rim shot* sound is used to create a sharper attack when playing backbeats in a groove or accents in a fill. To play a rim shot, hit the snare head and the snare rim at the same time with the same stick. (Check out the photo.)

Usually there is no special notation for the rim shot. Use your ear to decide if it fits the music you are playing.

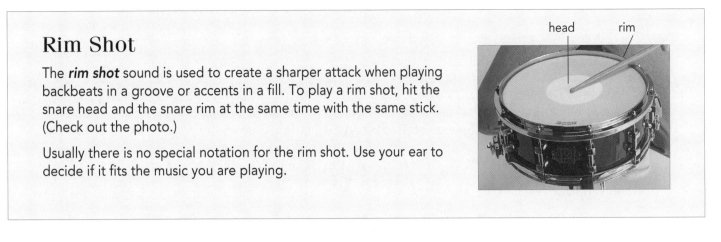

Try this example: Play the first measure normal, and the second measure with rim shots.

Track 67

Crackin' Quarters

Now hear how the rim shot sounds in the context of a beat.

Track 68

Shots Rang Out

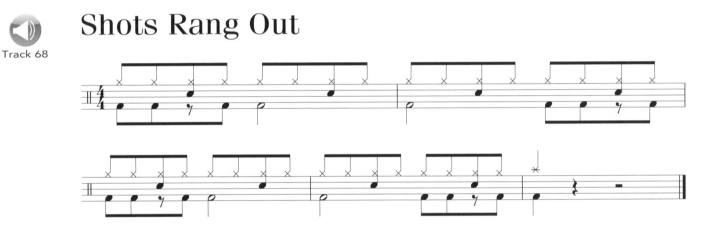

Now combine a few techniques for the next example. This starts with a sixteenth-note pickup fill using accents. Play the accents louder than the other notes as you just learned, and try to make them rim shots.

Track 69

Surfing the Wave

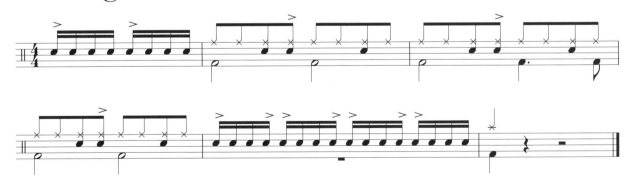

33

Flams

A great way to make a drum sound bigger and fatter is to play a **flam**. The flam consists of a *grace note* and a *main note*. The grace note is played softer and just before the main note. Start by holding your left stick about three inches above the head and your right stick ten inches. As you bring both sticks toward the head, the left should hit first (grace note), followed by the right (main note).

This is called a **right flam**. The flam is named after the main note. To play a left flam, simply reverse the sticking. The notes should be played close enough together so they sound as one note, but not exactly at the same time or they will produce what is called a "flat" flam.

First try some flams on the snare. Be sure to practice alternating so you can play them either way.

Track 70

Flam Bam

Flams can be played on the same drum or different drums. Here are some examples.

Track 71

Snare/Tom Flams

Flam Track

Track 72

Crash Cymbal Chokes

Grabbing the crash cymbal to stop it from ringing (after crashing) is known as **choking the cymbal**. This is useful in songs when the band stops abruptly and you don't want the cymbal to ring through. To choke the cymbal, hit the crash as you normally would with your right stick. Then, while still holding the stick in your left hand, use it to choke the cymbal with your thumb on top and the other fingers on the bottom.

A dot (·) above the cymbal crash will tell you to choke the cymbal.

Track 73

Using the Choke

It's time to try using all of the special techniques you just learned in a short song.

Track 74

Practice Pays Off

► Watch for beats, fills, and four-bar phrases.

35

Track 75

By now, you know that a quarter-note divided into two equal parts is two eighth notes. But what about a quarter note divided into three equal parts? That's a **triplet**:

Triplets are defined as "three notes that are played in the time of two notes of equal value." You can tell eighth-note triplets from "regular" eighth notes because the triplet eighths are beamed together with a number 3.

Here's how triplets are written and counted in 4/4 time.

Triplets are used in many styles of music, including blues, rock, and country. Here is a basic triplet-based beat played on the ride cymbal with a triplet fill at the end. The beat also sounds great on a closed hi-hat.

Track 76

Slow Blues

One popular triplet-based rhythm is the **shuffle**. The basic shuffle rhythm is obtained by leaving out (resting) the middle note of each three-note triplet group.

Track 77

Shuffling Along

Now use the shuffle pattern on the hi-hat in the next example.

Track 78

Shuffle the Deck

Previously you learned the one-measure repeat. You can also repeat two measures. The **two-measure repeat sign** looks like this:

Shuffles are also used in rock music, too. This example uses the shuffle in the bass drum.

Track 79

Heavy Foot

The typical jazz ride pattern also uses triplets. When playing jazz, the ride and hi-hat with the foot are the most dominant. The bass drum is used more for accenting and emphasizing. For coordination purposes, the next example uses quarter notes in the bass drum.

Track 80

Getting Jazzy

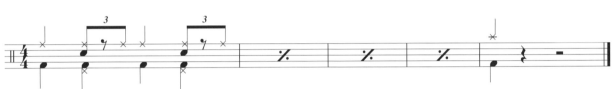

When playing jazz, left-hand snare coordination is a must. Try adding the following snare variations to the previous pattern. (In each of these, all parts are the same, except for the snare.)

Track 81

Snare Coordination #1

► Play the bass drum softly here for a "jazz" feel.

If you find these exercises difficult at first, play only the ride and snare parts. As you begin to feel comfortable with the patterns, try bringing in the hi-hat and/or bass drum until you're playing the complete beat.

Track 82

Snare Coordination #2

Track 83

Snare Coordination #3

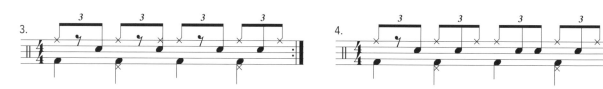

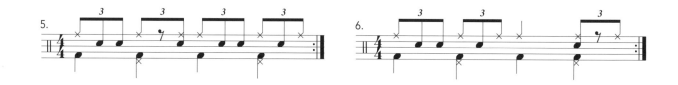

Do you realize that you're just two lessons away from completing the first half of *Play Drums Today!*? But there's still a lot more to come! For more music, be sure to check out the *Play Drums Today! Songbook*, which features real drum parts from many of your favorite songs.

More Beats & Fills

We've learned a lot of beats and a lot of fills; now let's concentrate on putting them together. Remember, as a drummer, your main job is to lay down a groove—but you also need to be able step out of that groove, adding fills now and again to make things exciting and to punctuate important spots in the music. Since most music is composed of four-bar phrases, you'll typically lay down a beat for about three measures or so, and then wrap up the phrase with a one-bar fill, like this:

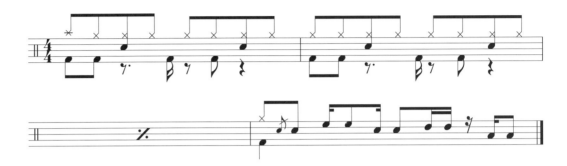

These next exercises are a great way to practice new fill ideas. They also help you begin to hear four-bar groupings, as you would in songs. The idea is to get you started making up your own fills. Play each three-measure beat as written, and then improvise a fill in the fourth measure. Then repeat, replacing the fill you just played with a different one each time. (You may want to review some of the fills you learned in Lesson 10 to get yourself started.)

These first four examples are in the rock style. Repeat each four times. To ensure your timing, we've included the "click" on the audio during the fourth measure. Remember to relax and not rush once you get to the fill.

Crazy Eighths

Rockin' Sixteenths

Off Beat

Hard Rock

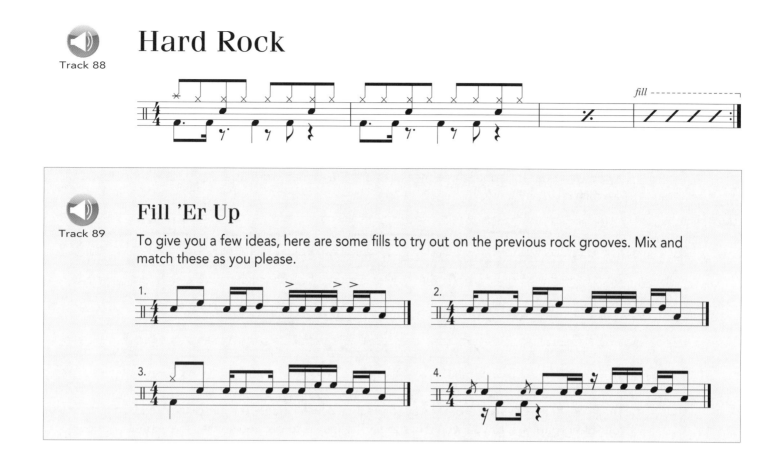

Fill 'Er Up

To give you a few ideas, here are some fills to try out on the previous rock grooves. Mix and match these as you please.

The next four examples are in the jazz and shuffle styles. Repeat each four times.

Pocket Shuffle

Swing It!

Doubling Up

Track 93

Kick Shuffle

Fill 'Er Up, Part 2

Track 94

Once again, here are a few fill ideas for you to work into the previous jazz and shuffle grooves. These are triplet-based:

Here's one more trick: Try working triplet-based fills into your rock grooves. Since the fill is a sort of break, the triplets work. They contrast with the main groove.

Track 95

With a Triplet Fill

3/4 Time

Although 4/4 meter is the most common time signature in music—including rock, blues, country, funk, and pop—it's not the *only* time signature. Another meter that turns up from time to time is **3/4**. That is, three beats (quarter notes) per measure.

count: 1   2   3

3/4 time feels very different from 4/4. Be sure to accent the first beat of each measure, just slightly; this will help you establish the feel.

Below are twelve grooves in 3/4 time. The first six are based on an eighth-note feel; the remainder use triplets. Each one is played twice, followed immediately by the next one. On your own, practice each one over and over until you can play it smoothly.

Take Three

Track 96

42

Basic Song Structures

Track 97

So far, you've learned lots of beats and fills. It's now time to put everything together into songs.

Most songs have different sections, which might include any or all of the following:

1. **Introduction** (or "intro"): This is a short section at the beginning that "introduces" the song to the listeners.

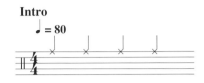

2. **Verse**: One of the main sections of the song. There will usually be several verses, each with different lyrics but all with the same music.

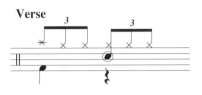

3. **Chorus**: Another main section of a song. There might be several choruses, but each chorus will usually have the same music, as well as the same lyrics (unlike the verse, in which the lyrics typically change).

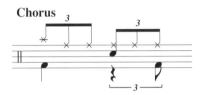

4. **Bridge**: This section makes a transition from one part of a song to the next, or serves as a break between sections. For example, you may find a bridge between the chorus and the next verse. You'll know the bridge when you hear it, because it feels like an entirely new section.

5. **Solo** (or **Interlude**): Solos are often played over the verse or chorus structure, but in some songs the solo section has its own structure. Solo sections are usually given to the guitar, keyboard, or sax players—and, every once in while, to the drummer.

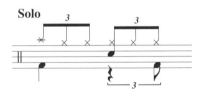

6. **Outro**: Similar to the "intro," this section brings the song to an end. Without an "outro," the song can end suddenly, or fade out. Any ending is fine, as long as it's believable and played with conviction.

When playing songs, you will usually play each verse the same, each chorus the same, etc., with only slight variations. This will signal the listeners as to the part of the song they are hearing.

Fills are most effective when played at the very end of a section. They serve as a signal that the song is about to go into a new section. Mark this new section with a cymbal crash (at the end of the fill). Crashes are sometimes also used to mark the halfway point of a section.

Now grab your sticks. This is the moment you've been practicing for. (Remember to have fun!)

Heartland Rock

Be sure to notice the similarities—and the differences—between each verse, each chorus, etc. Slight variations in each section keep things interesting.

These songs may challenge your reading skills. Take them slowly. Try to play at a pace that allows your eyes to read ahead in the music (by about a beat or so). This gives your hands and feet time to prepare.

Groovin' Blues

Chorus

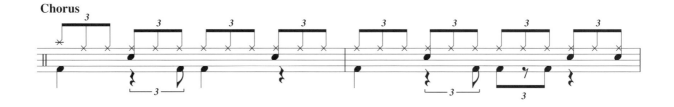

Solo

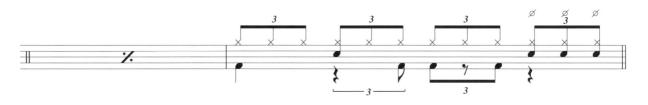

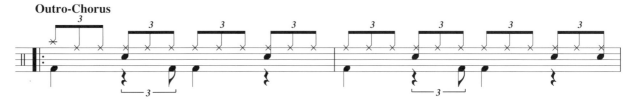

Outro-Chorus

Warm-Up

Track 100

The purpose of this section is to review some techniques and to warm up your hands and feet before you start practicing. Use this routine every time you sit down to play, before continuing with wherever you left off in the book.

Let's begin with a snare warm-up to get your hands moving from slow to fast, back to slow again.

Now play alternating sixteenth notes on the snare, and accent the notes marked.

Try rim shots on the snare to create a sharper attack sound. Play with the right stick for the first two measures; then with the left stick for the next two.

Flip your left stick around and play the cross-stick sound on beats 2 and 4.

Starting on the snare, alternate hands around the toms.

Play flams (hit one stick softer just before the other) on the snare and toms with the bass drum coordinated in between.

While keeping constant eighth notes going on the ride, practice alternating your feet and playing them together.

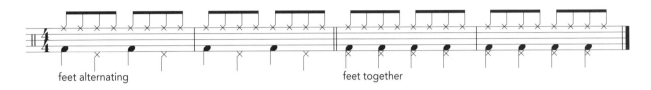

feet alternating   feet together

The ride cymbal produces different sounds when played on the bell and on the shoulder.

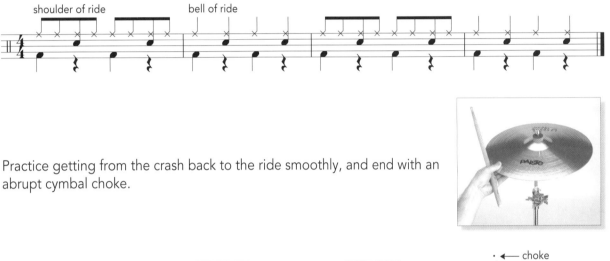

shoulder of ride   bell of ride

Practice getting from the crash back to the ride smoothly, and end with an abrupt cymbal choke.

• ← choke

Explore the different sounds possible on the hi-hat including closed, half-open, and open.

closed hats   half-open hats   open hats

foot hat

Get your hands working between the hi-hat and snare.

R L R L R L R L R L R L R L R L

Lesson 15 | # Rock 'n' Roll

Rock 'n' roll began in the '50s and drew from a variety of styles: mainly blues, R&B, and country—but also gospel, jazz, and folk. Some of its early pioneers included Chuck Berry, Elvis Presley, Little Richard, Jerry Lee Lewis, Buddy Holly, Bo Diddley, Bill Haley, the Everly Brothers, and Carl Perkins.

Straight Eighth-Note Rock

Let's begin with some straight eighth-note rock 'n' roll.

This is a fairly easy beat, and it sounds great. Just make sure to play the quarter-note snare and bass drum notes exactly together with the ride cymbal.

Track 101

► Notice the double snare hits on beat 4 of every other measure.

All Four Rock

In some ways, these next two beats are even easier, but you may need to practice the bass and snare drum parts to get comfortable with them.

Track 102

Drivin'

I Wonder
Track 103

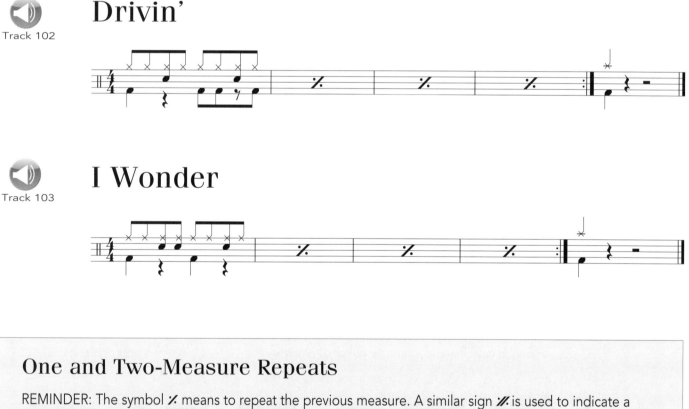

One and Two-Measure Repeats

REMINDER: The symbol ⁄. means to repeat the previous measure. A similar sign ⁄⁄. is used to indicate a two-measure repeat.

one-measure repeat

two-measure repeat

This groove is similar to "I Wonder" except that you're playing the mid tom. Watch that bass drum pattern, too.

Track 104

Two And

Now try this up-tempo rocker. Switching from eighth notes to quarter notes on the ride changes the feel on the second line.

Track 105

Faster Now

► Practice this one slowly at first. The sixteenth-note fills can be a challenge.

Shuffle-Based Rock

Much of the drumming on early rock 'n' roll records was based on the triplet feel; this is because many of the drummers playing this music were originally "swing" drummers. As you'll recall, the basic shuffle (a.k.a. "swing") rhythm is obtained by leaving out the middle note of a three-note triplet group:

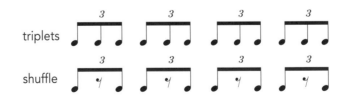

"Brown Shoes" is based on the shuffle rhythm played on the half-open hi-hat. The hi-hats should sound loose or "sloshy."

Brown Shoes

Track 106

▶ Again, practice these slowly at first, to get the shuffle feel.

For "Hot Dog," make sure that the second bass drum note is played in time with the ride cymbal. This can be tricky.

Hot Dog

Track 107

Try using this combination of tom-toms for "Susie Who?" Notice that the rhythm is similar to the last example, and yet it sounds quite different. The low tom carries the shuffle on beat 4.

Susie Who?

Track 108

You may find some of these beats difficult at first. If that's the case, and you get frustrated, take a break—or move on, and then come back to them later. Some things take time to process. When you return, you may be surprised to find that they've become a lot easier for you. (If not, just keep practicing!)

Occasionally in early rock 'n' roll, the drummer actually shuffles while the rest of the band plays straight eighth notes. Sound odd? Listen carefully to the next example, "Rollin' Train."

Rollin' Train

Track 109

The Shuffle Indication (♫ = ♩♪)

Shuffle notation can be hard to read. So instead, you'll often see shuffle or swing grooves written as straight eighth notes with the word "swing" or (♫ = ♩♪) written at the beginning of the music. This tells you to play all eighth notes with a shuffle feel.

Although they look different, both of the above examples would be played exactly the same. You can think of the sound as: "long-short, long-short, long-short, long-short."

Try "Places to Go." The snare drum is playing the shuffle rhythm with the left hand. Remember to play the accented notes louder.

Track 110

Places to Go

Breaking It Down

On challenging grooves, you may find it helpful to break the parts down and build your coordination gradually. For example, on "Places to Go," you could start with the snare and bass drum parts. Next, add a quarter-note ride cymbal (keep things simple at first). Then add the foot hi-hat on beats 2 and 4.

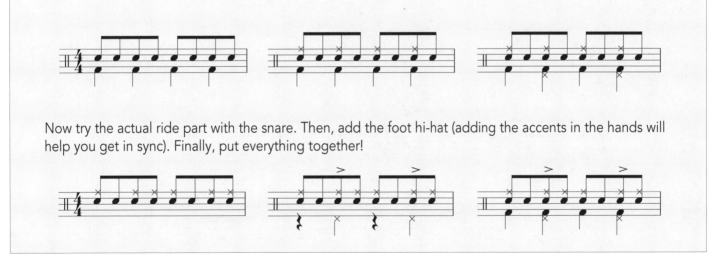

Now try the actual ride part with the snare. Then, add the foot hi-hat (adding the accents in the hands will help you get in sync). Finally, put everything together!

The Clave

Here's a fun beat in the style that Bo Diddley's drummer played in the '50s. It's based on a Latin pattern called a **clave**:

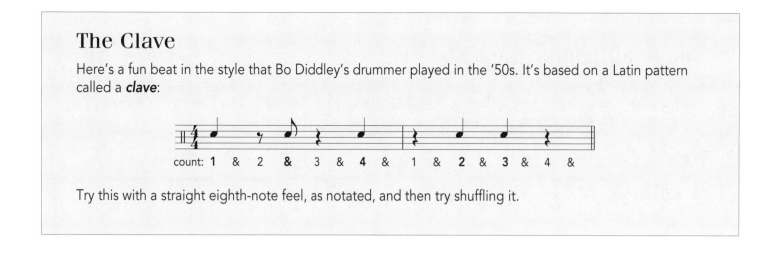

Try this with a straight eighth-note feel, as notated, and then try shuffling it.

Here's the shuffled version. The bass drum reinforces the clave pattern. The accents are everything!

Track 111

Shufflin' Floor Tom

Surf Rock

Surf rock began in the early '60s with reverb-drenched guitars played by artists like Dick Dale and the Surfaris. Later, bands like the Beach Boys and Jan & Dean added their original pop harmonies to further define this sound. The beat for this is typically driving, straight eighth-note-based.

Here's a fast one with a short snare fill every fourth measure. Remember four-bar phrasing?

Track 112

Wave Rider

► Be sure to play this one straight, *not* shuffled.

Four-Bar Phrases

Many songs are based on four-bar phrases. As a drummer, that means you'll typically lay down a groove for about three measures or so, and then add an improvised fill:

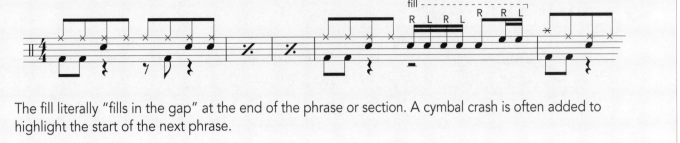

The fill literally "fills in the gap" at the end of the phrase or section. A cymbal crash is often added to highlight the start of the next phrase.

Sticking Principles

Hopefully, you noticed the "sticking" indications (e.g., RLRL) on some of the previous fills. These are included to help clear up any confusion you might have about how to play them. Good sticking is designed to help you play cleanly and easily—and to get you moving around the drums more quickly.

Let's practice our sticking with a few fills using just the snare drum. First, imagine you're playing alternating sixteenth notes beginning with your right stick:

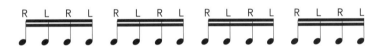

Now, for these next fills, keep that same sticking pattern (RLRL); however, if a note is skipped, so is its corresponding hand. You can try "air drumming" these hands if you like (play in the air, but don't hit anything) to keep the alternating sixteenths flowing, or not. This may seem awkward at first, but if you understand the principle, your drumming will be greatly enhanced:

The exception to the above "alternating sixteenths" rule is when playing consecutive eighth notes in a fill. Just alternate hands for the eighths, and then go back to alternating sixteenths:

Are you wondering why all of these fills lead with the right hand? Most fills are played around the toms from left to right, and leading with the right hand helps eliminate your sticks from crossing over. Don't be afraid to experiment on your own. Practice also leading with your left hand. Remember: when mixing up your fills between the snare and toms in a different order, they will require different stickings. Practice them until you find the most logical order.

To close this lesson, let's try a short rock 'n' roll song. This one starts with a drum fill on beat 3 of the pickup measure. On the track, you'll hear one full measure of count-off ("1, 2, 3, 4"), then two more clicks for the pickup measure ("1, 2"), and then you enter with the fill.

By the way, be sure to choke the crash cymbal at the end, for an abrupt finish.

Rockin' '50s

1st and 2nd Endings

You'll notice the above song has a **1st and 2nd ending** (indicated by brackets and the numbers "1" and "2"). The first time through the song, you should play the 1st ending, up until the repeat sign(:|)and then return to the initial repeat (|:) at the beginning of the song. The second time through, skip the 1st ending and jump to the 2nd ending, playing until the end of the song.

Country

Early country didn't include drums when it went commercial with its first record in the mid '20s; drums came into play much later—in the '50s. Of course, country music as we know it today commonly includes drums along with fiddle, banjo, dobro, steel guitar, acoustic and electric guitar, bass, harmonica, and mandolin.

Classic Country

Let's begin with some "classic country" beats. These are still used today on many recordings. The first is a two-beat feel with the accents on the "ands."

Track 114

Two Beat #1

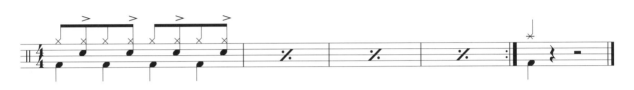

Now try a variation of the two-beat feel.

Track 115

Two Beat #2

Cut Time and the "Two-Beat" Feel

The two-beat feel gets its name because it's actually felt in *cut time*, or **2/2**, in which there are two beats in each measure. Here's how "Two-Beat #1" and "Two-Beat #2" would look in 2/2 time:

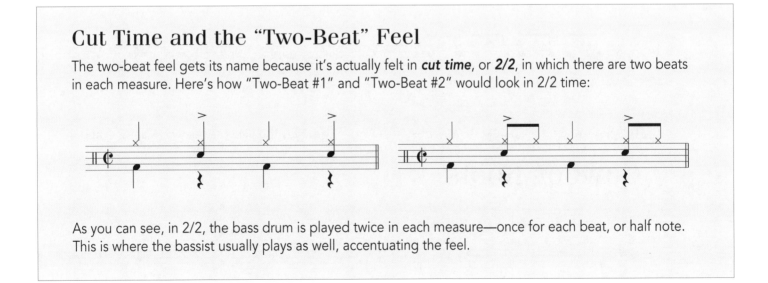

As you can see, in 2/2, the bass drum is played twice in each measure—once for each beat, or half note. This is where the bassist usually plays as well, accentuating the feel.

The "train beat" is named for its locomotive sound. It's played with alternating hands on the snare drum using sticks, brushes, or multi-rods. Play the unaccented snare notes much softer than the accented. This may take some practice to get the dynamics and the speed.

Steam Engine

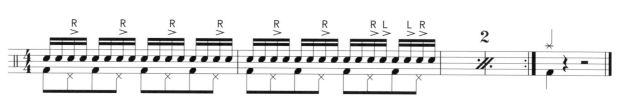

Brushes and Multi-Rods

Brushes and multi-rods are two popular alternatives to drumsticks that can add color to your playing. **Brushes** are much quieter than sticks and are typically used to vary the snare sound when playing country or jazz. The brush wires can also be dragged across the snare head, for a "stir" effect (this is why many snare heads have a white textured coating). **Multi-rods** also have a unique sound—louder than brushes but quieter than sticks. Made up of small wooden dowels wrapped together, multi-rods produce a loose, slapping sound.

This is another version of the train beat—this time, utilizing the shuffle. This is fun to play at all tempos. Once again, alternate your hands.

Shufflin' Snare

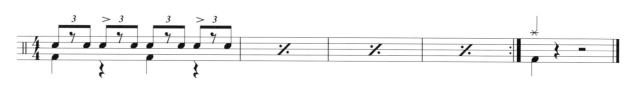

This is a more jazz-like beat in the "western swing" style. Play the accents heavy on beats 2 and 4.

Cowboy Boots

► Listen to the bassist's "walking line" on this track.

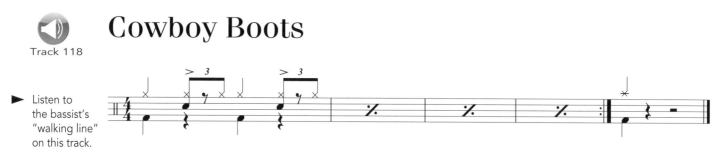

Many country tunes are in 3/4 time—usually referred to as a *waltz.* Try the next two examples using the cross-stick sound. The first is played straight, and the second is shuffled. Both of these are on the same track so you can hear the difference between the two feels.

Track 119

Gone To Texas

Lazy River

We promised you some fills for 3/4 time back in Lesson 13. So here they are—four with a straight eighth-note feel, and four with a shuffle feel. Once you've got these down, try inserting them into the fourth measure of each groove above, or into other 3/4 grooves.

Track 120

3/4 Fills

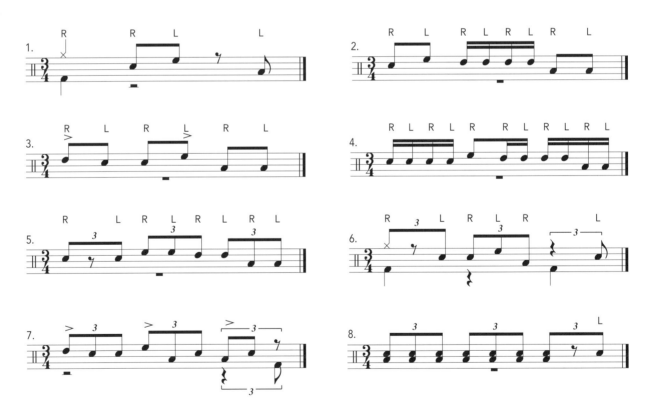

Contemporary Country

Contemporary country songs often favor a straight eighth-note feel, much like pop music.

Track 121

In the Pocket

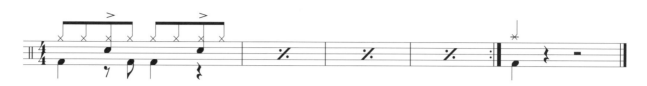

This beat is nice for a slower country ballad, again using the cross-stick.

Track 122

Leaving Home

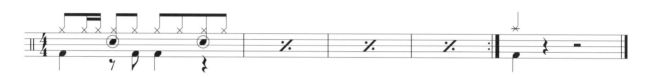

Contemporary country also uses the shuffle feel from time to time. Try these two variations at a moderate tempo.

Track 123

Rural Route

Cheatin'

"Ghost Town" is a shuffle ballad.

Track 124

Ghost Town

"Country Rock" uses cross-stick and tambourine for some textural variety. If you don't have a tambourine on your kit, just use cross-stick on the snare throughout.

Country Rock

Track 125

► The guitars on this track give the song a "rock" sound.

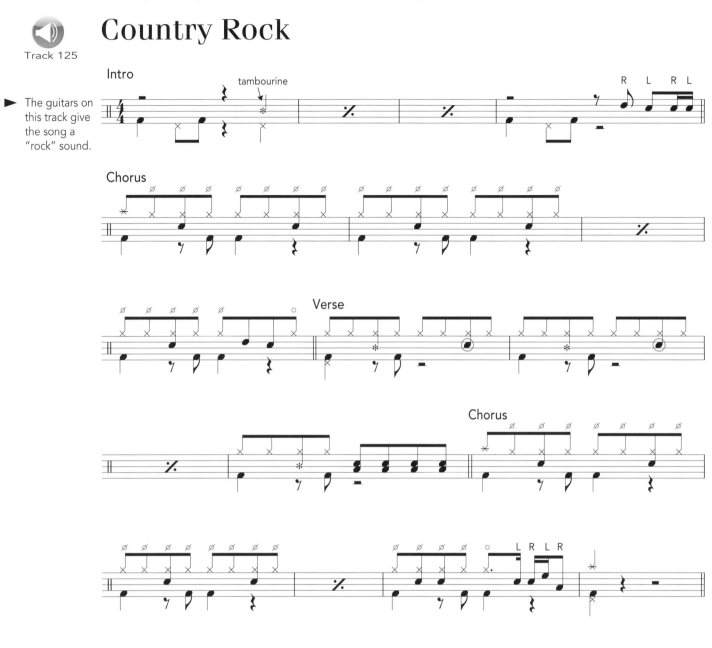

Tambourine

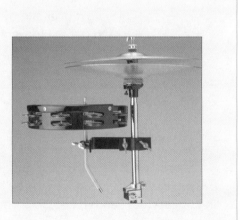

Drumset tambourine differs from hand-held tambourine because it's fitted with a special clamp to mount to your drums or cymbal stands. It can be placed anywhere on your drumset. Most commonly, tambourine is used as a substitute for snare hits on beats 2 and 4 in quieter passages, or to replace the hi-hat pattern for a different texture. Typically, it's played with a drumstick, but, for a softer attack, you can also hit it with your hand. Try adding tambourine to some beats you already know just for fun.

R&B

The original meaning of R&B was "rhythm and blues"—a form of music that evolved in the '40s, characterized by heavily syncopated dance rhythms and the use of blues scales. Later, R&B became a broader term for popular music that combined elements of blues, jazz, and rock 'n' roll.

Gospel

Gospel is a form of religious or inspirational music often played in an R&B style. Let's begin with a fun gospel groove played on the snare drum. Use alternate sticking, and be sure to accent beats 2 and 4. The hi-hat with foot consistently keeps time, but notice how the bass drum plays "off the beat" in measure 2. As always, begin slowly and speed up when you get the hang of it.

Track 126

Gospel Beat #1

This time, the right hand plays quarter notes on the hi-hat, and the left plays backbeats on the snare, again accenting beats 2 and 4. The bass drum plays the same part as in the previous example.

Track 127

Gospel Beat #2

If this groove gives you trouble, it's probably in the second measure. Try looping that measure—playing it over and over—very slowly, until you can play it continuously. Go as slow as you have to, just to get the movements down. Then try speeding it up. Finally, go back and try the whole groove again.

Syncopation

Playing "off the beat" is a way of adding rhythmic interest to a groove. The musical term for this is *syncopation*. It means "putting a strong note on a weak beat"—for example, playing or accenting the upbeats (the "ands") instead of the downbeats ("1," "2," "3," or "4").

Of course, we've been playing syncopated grooves for a while—we just didn't have a name for it yet!

Soul

Soul is another type of R&B—typically smoother, slicker, and a bit more commercial than pure rhythm 'n' blues. On the other hand, sometimes it can be gritty, too.

This one uses a popular bass drum pattern.

Track 128

The Standard

► Notice the open hi-hat before the repeat.

"Soulful" is a mid-tempo soul groove that uses **ghost notes.** These are notes that are barely played, but add quite a bit to the feel. The ghost notes appear in parentheses; play them softly. If you find it difficult to play them softly, then play them normally at first. Then work on ghosting them.

Track 129

Soulful

Here's a more relaxing triplet groove.

Track 130

Triplet Hat

The combination of open and closed hi-hat with the syncopated bass drum makes this one a challenge.

Track 131

Moderate R&B

Motown

The Motown sound—a bright, pop-oriented version of R&B—emanated in the '60s and '70s from the Detroit-based Motown Records. The name Motown was derived from the words "motor" and "town," a nickname for Detroit, which was a hub of the auto manufacturing industry. The sound consists of a strong backbeat, bouncy bass lines, and soulful vocals.

Track 132

Hat Shuffle

► Observe the shuffle indication on this groove.

"Sweet Sugar" uses a quarter-note pulse on the snare drum. This is a very popular Motown groove.

Track 133

Sweet Sugar

Listen to how the bass guitar follows the bass drum part in "Sunshine."

Track 134

Sunshine

Locking In

"Locking in" means listening to what the bassist is playing and being aware of how the bass and the drums work together to create a total groove. In fact, it's a good idea to have some concept of what the bass is playing—often, it will follow your bass drum pattern, or vice versa:

Offbeat Bass

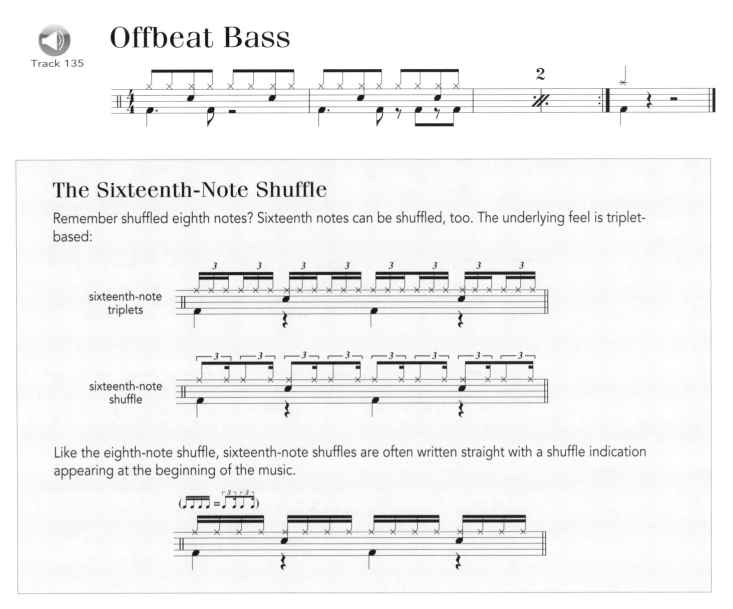

The Sixteenth-Note Shuffle

Remember shuffled eighth notes? Sixteenth notes can be shuffled, too. The underlying feel is triplet-based:

sixteenth-note triplets

sixteenth-note shuffle

Like the eighth-note shuffle, sixteenth-note shuffles are often written straight with a shuffle indication appearing at the beginning of the music.

"Emotional" uses shuffled sixteenth notes. Listen to the track before playing. (Keep in mind, only the sixteenths are shuffled; the eighths are straight.)

Emotional

Track 135

Track 136

Let's continue with the shuffled sixteenth feel on another short song. This song also includes ghost notes on the snare. It begins with a pickup fill; you'll hear three "clicks," then begin playing.

Track 137

The Preacher

► Notice the switch from the hi-hat to the ride, which changes the feel of each section.

Jazz and Blues

Jazz has been around for over 100 years. There are many different types of jazz, so we'll just touch on some of the basics to give you a better understanding of the general style.

For starters, you should know that the ride cymbal and hi-hat are the basis of timekeeping when playing jazz. The foot hat is typically used to accent beats 2 and 4, while the ride or hi-hat with stick play a shuffle pattern.

Swing

Swing is one of the original styles of jazz that caught on in the mid '30s with big bands such as Duke Ellington, Benny Goodman, and Count Basie.

Sometimes, all you need to play to hold the whole band together is the hi-hat. How about trying that right now?

Track 138

Swingin'

Try this one on the ride cymbal with your right hand, and play a cross-stick on beat 4 with your left hand.

Track 139

Playing Time

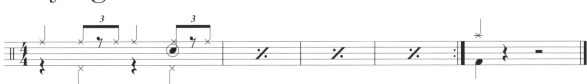

Next, let's add the snare and bass drum. These are played considerably softer than the cymbals in jazz or swing—especially in comparison to, say, rock 'n' roll—unless you're accenting certain musical phrases with the band.

Track 140

► Jazz is based around the quarter-note pulse.

Basic Jazz

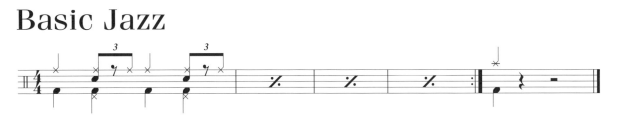

Quarter notes on the ride and with occasional swinging triplets are an effective approach to establishing the quarter-note pulse of jazz. "Broken Up" will give you an idea of this concept.

Track 141

Broken Up

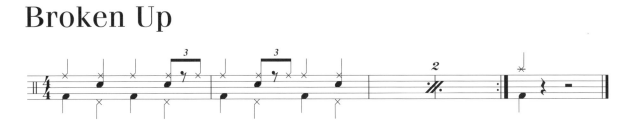

Improvisation

Jazz is an improvisational type of music—players compose "on the spot" around standard melodies or themes. When playing in a band situation, you would embellish upon these basic grooves by interacting with the other players spontaneously.

Try "Jazzy." This is how a typical improvised jazz drum part might look if written out.

Jazzy

Track 142

► Notice how the snare is played casually, off the beat, in the melody section.

For more ideas on improvisation, go back to the snare coordination exercises in Lesson 12. These are a great way of developing your improvisational chops.

Track 143

Rumba Boogie

Another fun jazz beat is the rumba boogie. This uses the cross-stick sound with the left hand, while the right hand plays normally. So, flip around your left stick for the cross-stick sound (play the tom using the butt end of the left stick) and follow the sticking indicated. This one begins with a sixteenth-note triplet starting on the "and" of beat 1. The real difficulty lies in getting from the cross-stick on the snare to the tom and back to the cross-stick smoothly.

For a full-set rumba that's less complex, try this next pattern. By the way, both of these rumba beats are played straight, not swung.

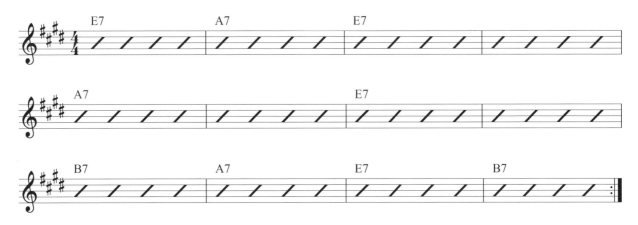

Blues

Blues evolved in the deep South from the spirituals and work songs of African-Americans in the early 1900s. Over the years, the blues branched out into many different sub-types that have their very own distinctions. We'll just touch on the basics here to get you started.

Part of what makes blues unique is its predictable structure—most commonly, blues songs follow what's called a ***12-bar form****. This doesn't mean that a song is only 12 bars (or measures) long, but rather, that it's based on a 12-bar chord progression, which repeats:

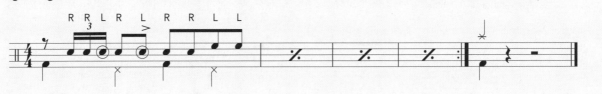

As a drummer, you don't need to know what chords are being played, but you should be able to hear the changes as they occur. Most importantly, you should realize that the 12-bar form consists of three four-bar phrases. (Look at the example above again if you didn't see this.) While you wouldn't likely insert a fill at the end of every four-bar phrase in a blues tune, you might choose to highlight the beginning of some phrases with a cymbal crash, and use a fill to mark the end of a 12-bar section.

*The 12-bar form is used in other styles as well. In fact, you've already played this as a rock 'n' roll progression in
  Lesson 1—remember "Rockin' '50s"?

Let's try some popular blues grooves in the shuffle style. These all use the 12-bar form. Listen to the audio to hear the progression.

Basic Shuffle

12/8 Time

Until now, you've been playing shuffle or swing grooves in 4/4 time. Another way they can be written, however, particularly slow ones, is in **12/8** time. In 12/8, there are twelve beats (or counts) per measure, and the eighth note receives one beat.

count: **1** 2 3, **4** 5 6, **7** 8 9, **10** 11 12

Notice above that the eighth notes are grouped into threes—much like triplets. That's because the underlying pulse is actually a dotted quarter note; beats 1, 4, 7, and 10—the first note of each three-note group—are accented. For example, compare the following two beats: One is written as triplets in 4/4, the other as eighth notes in 12/8. (They both sound the same.)

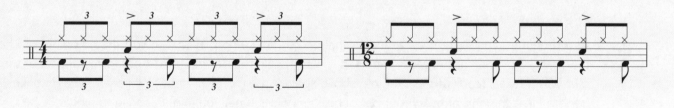

Eighth notes in the hi-hat plus a very active shuffle pattern in the kick drum give this 12/8 beat a very distinctive feel. Take it slow.

Track 145

Slow Blues

Now the shuffle pattern is on the ride. Add snare hits on the "and" of each quarter note and a four-to-the-bar kick drum pattern with foot hat on beats 2 and 4, and you've got a challenging, but unique upbeat blues groove.

Track 146

Upbeat

Here are six more blues grooves. You'll hear each one played twice, followed by the next (with a measure of four "clicks" in between). Any of these could be extended to create a 12-bar blues.

More Beats

Ghostless Beats

The ghost notes are what make many of the previous beats cool, but to make them easier, we've taken them out for practice. Since #3 doesn't have any, and #4 and #5 would be the same without them, there's only four left.

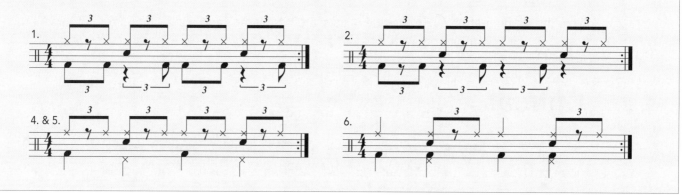

Following a Chart

On the next page, you'll see a basic blues chart, sometimes referred to as a "road map." Charts are useful for musicians playing a song together for the first time. They provide a quick overview of crucial aspects of the song—like its form, its chord progression, its style, tempo, etc.

For example, looking at this chart, you should recognize that the song is a 12-bar blues in three sections. The first section is a keyboard melody; the second, a guitar solo; the third, a repeat of the keyboard melody. The time signature (4/4) and the tempo and style (moderate shuffle) are also provided, giving you an idea of the overall feel of the song.

Interpreting a chart like this requires some creativity. The notation used—called **slash notation**—is very general. Each slash represents one beat in the current time signature and simply means that you should play something—anything—during that measure. Whatever you play, it would make sense that you continue in a similar style throughout the song. It would also make sense to highlight different sections by adding some variation—for example, playing on the hi-hat during the first and third sections, and switching to the ride for the guitar solo in the second section. (You would not, however, normally switch in the middle of a 12-bar section.)

There are purposely no drums on this track. Try all six examples from "More Beats," putting them into this chart and jamming with the band. You may want to insert a short fill at the end of each 12 bars to indicate that the form is about to start over or to end the song. Since this is a shuffle, it would make sense for your fills to be based on quarter notes or triplets (rather than straight eighths or sixteenth notes). Have fun playing these, and feel free to make up some of your own grooves to fit the song.

Open Blues Jam

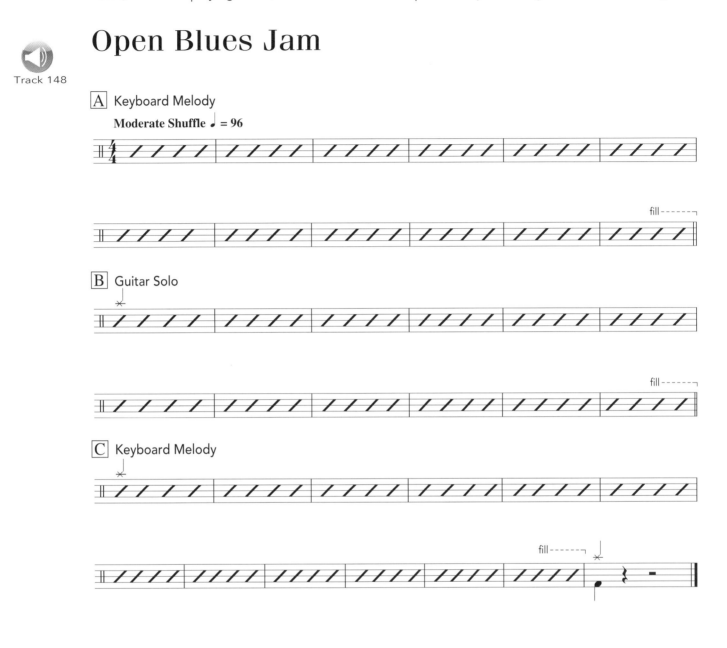

Just for a few ideas, here are some half-measure, shuffle-based fills. Try inserting any of these into your "Open Blues Jam."

Half-Measure Fills

Modern Rock

Compared to early rock 'n' roll, modern rock—from the late '60s up to today—is more often straight eighth-note based rather than shuffled. The bass drum is generally busier, and the hi-hat (played with sticks) is used for the majority of the beats. Let's touch on a few of the dominant modern rock styles.

Hard Rock

Hard rock was strong from the late '60s through the '80s and could be described as loud, simple, and driving—with the help of the distorted guitar sound.

Keeping it simple doesn't have to be boring. Try "digging in" on this example using the half-open hi-hat sound.

Track 150

Solid

Accents on the Hi-Hat

A technique used to help drive the eighth-note pulse in modern rock is accenting beats 1, 2, 3, and 4 on the hi-hat. Typically, these accents are implied rather than notated.

Track 151

► Accent beats 1, 2, 3, and 4 on the hi-hat here.

Straight Forward

Sometimes it's very effective to play eighth notes on the floor tom instead of the hi-hat to help drive the beat along.

Track 152

Drivin'

Syncopated Sixteenths

The use of sixteenth notes in the next song is another example of **syncopation**, the placement of rhythmic accents on weak beats or weak portions of beats—in this case, the "e" of beat 3 on the snare, and the "a" of beats 2 and 3 on the bass drum.

Track 153

Syncopated

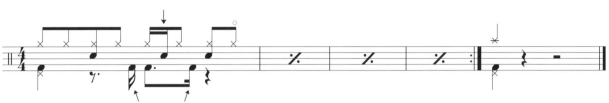

Alternative

In the early '90s, bands like Nirvana, Pearl Jam, and Soundgarden helped forge a new style of rock known as "alternative." Gone were the guitar solos of the '80s and in their place came a more stripped-down, textural approach to the instrument. Drums became a little busier, with straight eighth-note grooves giving way to frequent ghost notes and sixteenths.

This example is notated with the open hi-hat since the sound should be more than half-open. With your left foot on the hi-hat pedal, press down just enough so that the cymbals "sizzle" together when you're playing this very loudly. This one moves along pretty quickly; take it slowly to start with.

Track 154

Bashing

"Offbeat" makes good use of ghost notes. If playing these ghost notes is too difficult at first, take them out and practice the groove without them, playing the snare on beats 2 and 4 only.

Track 155

Offbeat

Now play straight sixteenth notes with your right stick on the hi-hat. Just line up the bass drum notes under the corresponding hi-hat notes to ensure the evenness. Notice when the open hi-hats occur and when to close them with your left foot.

Steady

Sometimes, drummers use the crash cymbal to ride on. This technique has been around for quite some time, but it's been growing even more popular since the early '90s through today. Play on the edge of the crash cymbal, as you normally would, but continue, as in this case, with eighth notes. This creates a "shhh" sound, rather than the more defined sound of the closed hi-hat or even the ride.

It's common to accent the downbeats to help create the underlying quarter-note pulse. Try this on "Crash Riding."

Crash Riding

Punk

"Back to the basics" describes what punk rock is all about. It's just louder, faster, and more abrasive than any other rock 'n' roll. It thrives on few chords and simple melodies. Some early punk bands included the Ramones and the Sex Pistols. Two of the more modern punk bands are Green Day and Rancid. These examples look simple, but it's all about playing fast with lots of endurance.

Fast

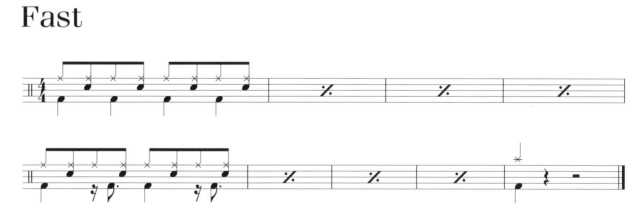

This one really gets your bass drum foot going.

Track 159

Faster

The quarter-note pulse on the snare drum really drives this one along.

Track 160

Fastest

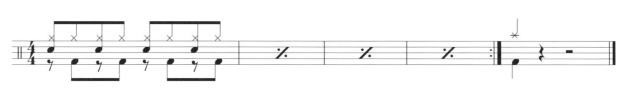

For a more "abrasive" sound, use the open hi-hat. Remember that you still want some "sizzle" to the hi-hat sound while you're playing it loud.

Track 161

Noise

► Start with the hi-hat and snare, then add the bass drum.

Take your time working out the syncopated bass drum part for this one before attempting to play it fast. Again, you might want to "lock in" on the hi-hat and snare pattern first.

Track 162

Out of Control

Metal

Metal (sometimes referred to as "heavy metal") is a form of rock music similar to hard rock, but technically more challenging. The songs are usually assembled around the guitar riff. The rhythms can be quite rigid with an almost military feel.

Track 163

Steel

For this example, the drum groove is very similar to the punk beats in the last section. The stylistic difference lies in the more technical guitar part.

Heavy

Track 164

The difficulty in this example is playing the offbeat bass drum pattern. Notice that the last sixteenth bass drum note is played right into beat 1 of the repeat, making it even more challenging to play this one fast.

Defiance

Track 165

► Here's another groove that rides on the crash cymbal.

Half Time

The next example, "Rigid," uses a half-time feel. Notice that the snare backbeat is on 3 instead of beats 2 and 4, which gives it this feel. Here is a comparison between the two.

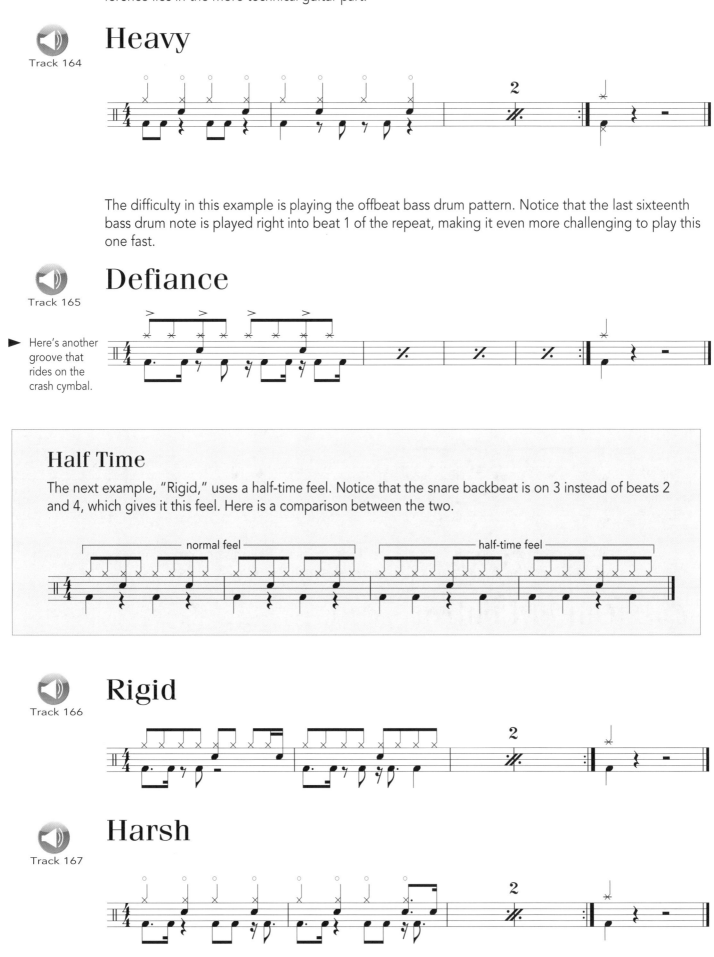

Rigid

Track 166

Harsh

Track 167

Double Bass

Double bass drum playing started in the jazz and swing era but is now used mostly in modern rock and metal. Originally, "double bass" meant literally playing two bass drums—one with each foot. But with the advancement of bass drum pedals in the '80s, the double pedal became a more affordable way to play both beaters on one bass drum, eliminating the need to haul around an extra drum.

Having a double bass pedal isn't a necessity—many great drummers play without one. And you might not have one on your current kit. However, they do offer some advantages, allowing you to play faster on the bass drum by using both feet and making it easier to play for extended periods without tiring as quickly.

To give you a taste of what's possible, here are some popular double bass patterns. The left foot bass drum is notated on the lowest line of the staff. If you don't have a double pedal, try playing these grooves anyway (play both parts with just your right foot).

Track 168

Drivin' Eighths

This is similar to the last example, but it sounds a little less driving without playing the bass drum on 2 and 4.

Track 169

Less Driving

This is a classic double bass drum pattern—great for coordination and endurance. If you're practicing without a double bass pedal here, substitute your left foot on the hi-hat pedal. (In the right hand, instead of a half-open hi-hat, play the ride cymbal.)

Track 170

All Feet

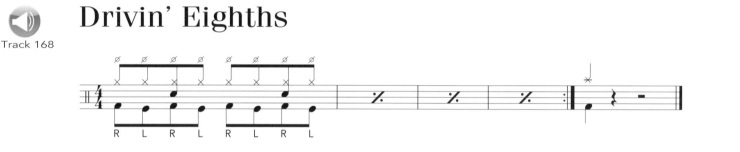

Now try triplets with your feet. Notice beats 1 and 3 are played with the right foot, 2 and 4 with the left.

Track 171

Heavy Foot

Sometimes it's fun to play short bursts of bass drum notes. It's usually easier to play these faster since you can rest in between groups of notes.

Track 172

Speed Metal

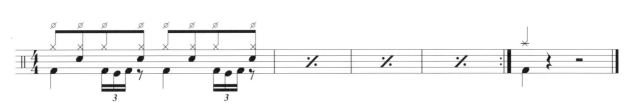

Many times, it's possible to play grooves like the next one with only one foot, but using both feet allows you to make both sixteenth notes sound strong. You'll be able to play this faster, too.

Track 173

Broken Up

This has two quick bass drum notes just before beat 4. In case you're wondering, the three beams make them thirty-second notes ($\|$:).

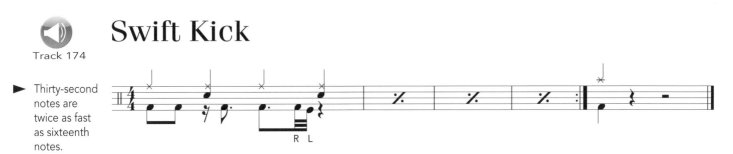
Track 174

Swift Kick

► Thirty-second
notes are
twice as fast
as sixteenth
notes.

The Bounce

If you don't have a double bass pedal, you can still play many of the previous grooves—in particular, any with just two sixteenth kicks in a row ( )—using a technique called the **bounce.** The bounce is based on the "heel up" approach to playing bass drum—using the ball of your foot on the pedal (heel up) and letting your whole leg come down, pivoting from the hip (as opposed to keeping the foot flat and using your ankle for this motion).

Try this: Begin playing as you normally would, with your heel up, but instead of letting the ball of your foot remain on the pedal as you bring your leg down, drop your heel first—letting it depress the pedal—and then roll your foot forward so that the ball of your foot plays a second note. It's sort of a two-part "rocking" motion: 1) heel, 2) ball.

hit #1: heel

hit #2: ball

You may want to imagine *lifting* up the ball of your foot as you strike with the heel, then *rolling forward.* (It's sort of a "skipping" motion.) It may also help to practice this with your shoes off so you can feel the pedal better.

Double bass is a great way to spice up your fills. The following examples use sixteenth notes and eighth-note triplets. Play each one twice with a measure of "clicks" in between. Make them flow as evenly as possible. (Try using the bounce for any fills that use just two kicks in a row.)

Track 175

Sixteenth Fills

Triplet Fills

Odd Time

So far we've covered 4/4, 3/4, and 12/8 time. The next song features a new time signature—6/4. There are six beats in a measure, and the quarter note receives one beat. This is considered "odd time." Other "popular" odd time signatures include 5/4 and 7/4.

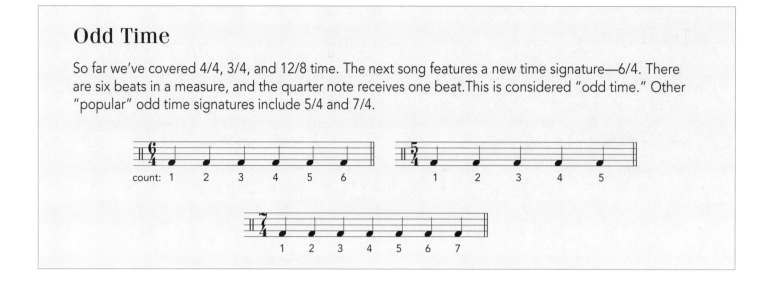

Be sure to count along as you play this one. Notice the time signature changes to 4/4 during the chorus, then back to 6/4 for the outro.

Track 176

► You'll hear six clicks on the count-in for this song.

Strangely Odd

Funk

In the late '60s, soul and rock began to mix to form a new style called "funk." James Brown and Sly Stone were the godfathers of funk; George Clinton and his bands Parliament/ Funkadelic represented the next breed of funksters.

Classic Funk

What makes funk beats so "funky" are the offbeat snare hits, ghost notes, and open hi-hats. Take your time with these; they can be quite tricky at first. Be aware of the accents and ghost notes. The dynamics between limbs make all the difference in the way these feel.

Everything happens here on beat 3.

Slight Funk

Track 177

This fun example uses a very syncopated snare part. Even though it looks complicated, the hi-hat just plays straight eighth notes, and the snare notes fall in between. Play those accents!

Funky

Track 178

Funk beats often uses ghost notes, and this is a great example. The open hi-hats also make it interesting.

Ghosting

Track 179

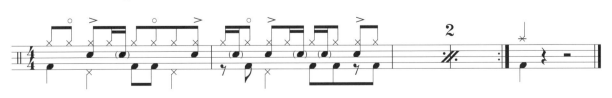

Playing the last snare note on the "and" of 4 in the first measure creates a lull in the feeling of this groove. There are those ghost notes again!

Freezing

Track 180

Funk Rock

Funk rock, as the name implies, is a merger of "funk" and "rock" genres. The syncopated feel of the drums and the distorted guitar sound define this style.

The notes here are all simple, but they're not necessarily where you might expect them. Play this with conviction.

Quarter Funk

Modern rock beats tend to have quite a few bass drum kicks in them. When you mix this with funk, you wind up with quite a few notes to play!

Plenty of Notes

Funk Metal

Take the popping bass lines and syncopated rhythms of funk, combine them with the loud guitars and riffs of heavy metal, and you've got funk metal.

The syncopation happens more in the bass drum part of the following examples, rather than the snare, as in the classic funk beats.

Frenzy

Anger

Choppy

New Orleans

Many musical historians believe that all contemporary funk came from the New Orleans "second line" parade beat feel. The following are two basic second line patterns. Play each of these with alternating strokes on the snare drum.

In "Street March," play accents on the snare along with the bass drum rhythm.

Street March

Track 186

By changing the accents on the snare to beats 2 and 4, the feel of this similar pattern is now changed.

New Orleans Backbeat

Track 187

Disco

Disco originated from the groove-oriented sound of the '70s and funk. Disco is all about keeping a simple beat to dance to. A frequent sound is the open and closed hi-hat.

Try these popular disco patterns.

Nightlife

Track 188

Hip-Hop

Hip-hop is a type of funk that evolved from rap music. The shuffle indication in parentheses (♪♪♪ = ♪♪♪) tells you to shuffle the sixteenth notes.

Hip-Hop #1

Hip-Hop #2

Paradiddles

You may remember in Lesson 11 learning to play flams. These were an example of a **rudiment**—a specific sticking used to create a particular rhythmic pattern or effect. Another fun and useful rudiment is the "paradiddle."

A **single paradiddle** is a group of four evenly spaced notes (usually eighths or sixteenths) that are played with two alternating strokes followed by a double stroke. Often, you'll play two paradiddles in a row, as in the following example:

Practice this pattern until you can play it effortlessly and don't have to think about the sticking. Accenting the beginning of each four-note group makes it easier to hear the paradiddles. If it helps, try saying the name of the rudiment as you play it:

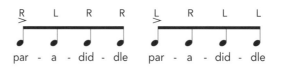

par - a - did - dle   par - a - did - dle

Now try adding the bass drum and playing your paradiddles faster.

86

Now try the *double paradiddle*. Just add two more alternating single strokes at the beginning of each single paradiddle, and you have double paraddidles.

Lastly, try the *triple paradiddle*. You guessed it: Add two alternating strokes to the beginning of each double paradiddle.

Practice all three of these until they become smooth and second nature to you. Another fun way to practice paradiddles is by playing them on the drumset using the toms too.

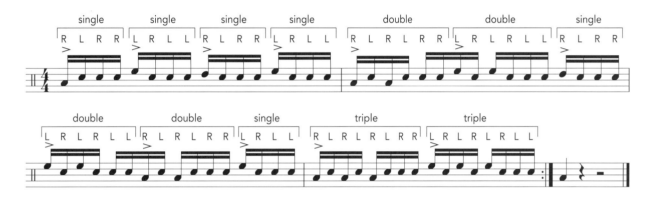

Here are a couple useful funk beats that use paradiddles. Keep your right stick on the hi-hat and your left on the snare. For starters, play all of the hi-hat and snare notes at the same volume. When you become more confident, play the ghost notes soft and the accents loud for the true feel of these grooves. These may look frightening at first—until you understand the concept.

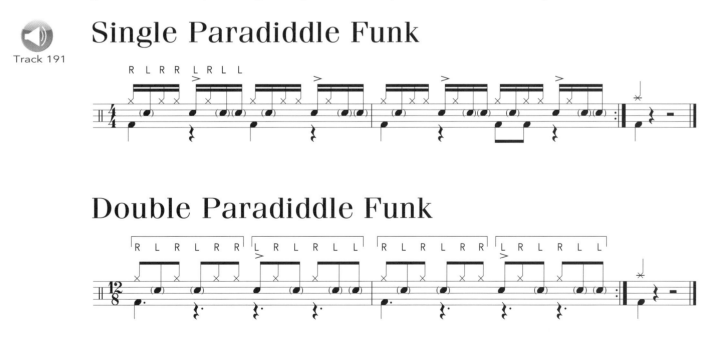

Single Paradiddle Funk

Track 191

Double Paradiddle Funk

To close this lesson, we'll end with a short song incorporating paradiddles along with other funk beats and fills. Practice this song in sections first, before playing it all together.

Feeling Funky

Track 192

Latin

Let's touch on some popular Latin rhythms. These are fun to play and will help build your coordination.

Samba

The samba is Brazilian in origin. It's a faster Latin style, often felt in "two" rather than "four."

Try playing this pattern on the bell of the ride cymbal (if you have a cowbell, use that as a substitute). Your left hand will play the cross-stick and reach up to then play the tom. After playing the tom, try to set the stick down quietly on the snare to play the cross-stick again.

Samba Bell

Track 193

If you find "Samba Bell" difficult, try practicing just the feet. This is the standard samba foot pattern:

Then try the same beat as above but with an eighth-note ride.

"Straight-Eighth Samba" features a popular samba clave on cross-stick. Remember the **clave**? It's a distinctive rhythm found in Latin music. Actually, it's more than just one rhythm—there are different clave patterns for different styles.

Straight-Eighth Samba

Track 194

▶ The clave (on cross-stick) should sound almost like a separate percussionist.

Bossa Nova

The bossa nova is another popular Brazilian rhythm that has been used by both rock and jazz bands. It's an outgrowth of the samba and usually has a slow to moderate 4/4 feel.

The cross-stick often imitates the sound of the clave rhythm. Try "The Bossa" and then "Reverse Bossa," which reverses the clave pattern played with the cross-stick.

The Bossa

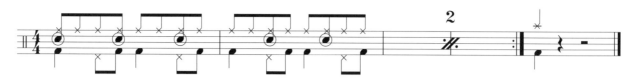

Reverse Bossa

Mambo

Mambo is an Afro-Cuban dance style with a medium to up-tempo feel.

The mambo uses a broken right-hand pattern instead of steady eighth notes; this sounds great on the ride cymbal bell or on a cowbell. You may want to practice this groove starting with the left hand and feet parts first, adding the right-hand ride when you're comfortable.

Let's Mambo

Cowbell

Cowbell is another percussion instrument you might want to add to your drumkit. It's a popular substitute for the ride cymbal and can also be used for solos or "breakdowns." In fact, if you have an extra pair of hands in your band, the cowbell is a great instrument on which to have the vocalist or another percussionist play the clave pattern.

Cha-Cha

Cha-cha is also Afro-Cuban in origin, and usually has a moderate 4/4 feel.

Eighth notes on the hi-hat, along with cross-stick quarter notes, help to drive this beat along.

Cha-Cha, Anyone?

Expanding Your Drumset

We've covered all the parts of a standard drumset—so you're ready to play just about anything.

The more you play drums, the more you'll discover what you like and what you don't. Eventually, you'll want to customize your kit; every drummer does. You may want more toms, more cymbals, more gadgets—or you may want less. Here are a few options to consider for the future.

Splash cymbals
A great effect for quiet playing or for solos.

China cymbal
Another nice effect.

Cowbell
Substitute it for the hi-hat or ride for a harder or more exotic sound.

Fixed hi-hat
For a closed hi-hat sound when both feet are busy.

Tambourine
Another, brighter hi-hat substitute.

Tom-toms
More toms give you more choices for improvising. Fewer toms keep things simple.

Double bass pedal
Allows you to play faster eighths or sixteenths with both feet.

You don't need any of these extras to have fun making music, though. So keep playing, and enjoy yourself!

Changing Your Drumheads

If you've played through this book—or you've been playing drums for a while—you may notice that your drumheads are beginning to show some "wear and tear." Over time, drumheads stretch out and begin to lose their tone. If your drums came with white-coated heads and you can now see through them where you play a lot, or if they have dents, you may want to consider buying new heads. It's best to change all of your tom heads at the same time. The snare drum head might need to be changed more often since it's usually played much more.

What Type of Heads Do I Need?

Drumheads come in all different brands and types. If you bought your drumset new, typically it would come fitted with single-ply heads (because of their versatility). If you consider yourself mainly a rock drummer and play hard, you may want to try two-ply heads for your toms. Two-ply drumheads will last longer and produce a more muffled and deep tone. This applies to the bass drum as well. Before buying heads at your local drum store, talk to other, more experienced drummers about what they prefer.

To figure out what size drumheads you need, measure the diameter of each drum *inside* the metal hoop. You are actually measuring the drum shell. A typical five-piece drumset consists of a 22" bass drum, 14" snare, and 12", 13", and 16" toms. The measurements should always be rounded to the nearest inch. If you're not sure, take your drums along with you when buying heads, just to be safe.

Removal and Cleaning

Once you've decided on which heads to purchase, you'll now have to change them. If you're changing your tom heads, take the toms off of the drumset and place them on a carpeted floor in order from small to large. When removing the worn-out heads, take your drum key (the special tool that fits on the tension rods—the screws that tension down the drumhead on the shell) and turn counterclockwise on each rod to loosen the head. It's a good idea to turn each one just a little at a time—rather than loosening one rod completely before moving on to the next—to avoid uneven stress on the drum shell. This is especially true on snare drums, since they're usually tensioned the tightest. You don't need to remove the tension rods from the hoop; just let them dangle as you pull the head and hoop off the drum shell. At this point, you may want to remove any dust or foreign matter that possibly has accumulated inside the drum. As long as the head is off, take a screwdriver and lightly tighten the screws on the inside of the shell that may have loosened from the vibrations during playing. Be careful not to over-tighten the screws.

Installation and Tuning

Now take the new drumhead and place it on the drum. Separate the hoop from the old head and place it on the new head. Rethread the tension rods into the lugs with your fingers—being careful not to cross-thread—until they are finger-tight.

If your new head has a logo, start with the tension rod just to the right and tighten it a half turn. Now tighten the opposite rod the same. Then move to the next rod just to the right of where you first started and continue in the same fashion until you've tightened each a half turn. Now use the same pattern to give each rod another half turn all the way around the drum. Place your palm in the middle of the drum and put your other hand on top of that. Press down the head in the middle three or four times to stretch it in a little. You may hear a cracking sound (the drumhead resin settling) while doing this. This is normal. Take a drumstick and tap about an inch in from the hoop on the head at each tension point. Listen to the pitch of each. The object

is to make them the same. Take your drum key and begin to tighten or loosen to make them match in pitch. If you are tuning the toms right now, you may be pretty close to the desired tension. Snare

drumheads are commonly tuned higher, so after matching the pitch at each rod, you may need to go around the drum again once or twice to reach the desired pitch.

Use this same procedure for all of the toms. After that point, you'll want to listen to the relationship in pitch between the different toms, so that no two drums are too close in pitch. If they are too close, using your drum key, repeat the same procedure to bring up or down the head of your choice. A head tuned quite low will feel flabby and make it more difficult to play fast fills, but tune mostly for the desired pitch you are looking for.

If you have toms with both top and bottom heads, you'll need to flip over the drum and tune those, too. Use the same tuning procedure on each bottom head, either matching the pitch to the top head or slightly higher. Don't be afraid to experiment. Tuning drums can be difficult and personal. It's not as easy as plugging a guitar into an electronic tuner. Take your time and practice this.

Play Today! Series

The Ultimate Self-Teaching Series

These are complete guides to the basics, designed to offer quality instruction, terrific songs, and professional-quality audio with tons of full-demo tracks and instruction. Each book includes over 70 great songs and examples!

Play Accordion Today!
00701744	Level 1 Book/Audio	$10.99
00702657	Level 1 Songbook Book/Audio	$12.99

Play Alto Sax Today!
00842049	Level 1 Book/Audio	$9.99
00842050	Level 2 Book/Audio	$9.99
00320359	DVD	$14.95
00842051	Songbook Book/Audio	$12.95
00699555	Beginner's – Level 1 Book/Audio & DVD	$19.95
00699492	Play Today Plus Book/Audio	$14.95

Play Banjo Today!
00699897	Level 1 Book/Audio	$9.99
00701006	Level 2 Book/Audio	$9.99
00320913	DVD	$14.99
00115999	Songbook Book/Audio	$12.99
00701873	Beginner's – Level 1 Book/Audio & DVD	$19.95

Play Bass Today!
00842020	Level 1 Book/Audio	$9.99
00842036	Level 2 Book/Audio	$9.99
00320356	DVD	$14.95
00842037	Songbook Book/Audio	$12.95
00699552	Beginner's – Level 1 Book/Audio & DVD	$19.99

Play Cello Today!
00151353	Level 1 Book/Audio	$9.99

Play Clarinet Today!
00842046	Level 1 Book/Audio	$9.99
00842047	Level 2 Book/Audio	$9.99
00320358	DVD	$14.95
00842048	Songbook Book/Audio	$12.95
00699554	Beginner's – Level 1 Book/Audio & DVD	$19.95
00699490	Play Today Plus Book/Audio	$14.95

Play Dobro Today!
00701505	Level 1 Book/Audio	$9.99

Play Drums Today!
00842021	Level 1 Book/Audio	$9.99
00842038	Level 2 Book/Audio	$9.95
00320355	DVD	$14.95
00842039	Songbook Book/Audio	$12.95
00699551	Beginner's – Level 1 Book/Audio & DVD	$19.95
00703291	Starter	$24.99

Play Flute Today
00842043	Level 1 Book/Audio	$9.95
00842044	Level 2 Book/Audio	$9.99
00320360	DVD	$14.95
00842045	Songbook Book/Audio	$12.95
00699553	Beginner's – Level 1 Book/Audio & DVD	$19.95

Play Guitar Today!
00696100	Level 1 Book/Audio	$9.99
00696101	Level 2 Book/Audio	$9.99
00320353	DVD	$14.95
00696102	Songbook Book/Audio	$12.99
00699544	Beginner's – Level 1 Book/Audio & DVD	$19.95
00702431	Worship Songbook Book/Audio	$12.99
00695662	Complete Kit	$29.95

Play Harmonica Today!
00700179	Level 1 Book/Audio	$9.99
00320653	DVD	$14.99
00701875	Beginner's – Level 1 Book/Audio & DVD	$19.95

Play Mandolin Today!
00699911	Level 1 Book/Audio	$9.99
00320909	DVD	$14.99
00115029	Songbook Book/Audio	$12.99
00701874	Beginner's – Level 1 Book/Audio & DVD	$19.99

Play Piano Today!
Revised Edition
00842019	Level 1 Book/Audio	$9.99
00298773	Level 2 Book/Audio	$9.95
00842041	Songbook Book/Audio	$12.95
00699545	Beginner's – Level 1 Book/Audio & DVD	$19.95
00702415	Worship Songbook Book/Audio	$12.99
00703707	Complete Kit	$22.99

Play Recorder Today!
00700919	Level 1 Book/Audio	$7.99
00119830	Complete Kit	$19.99

Sing Today!
00699761	Level 1 Book/Audio	$10.99

Play Trombone Today!
00699917	Level 1 Book/Audio	$12.99
00320508	DVD	$14.95

Play Trumpet Today!
00842052	Level 1 Book/Audio	$9.99
00842053	Level 2 Book/Audio	$9.95
00320357	DVD	$14.95
00842054	Songbook Book/Audio	$12.95
00699556	Beginner's – Level 1 Book/Audio & DVD	$19.95

Play Ukulele Today!
00699638	Level 1 Book/Audio	$10.99
00699655	Play Today Plus Book/Audio	$9.99
00320985	DVD	$14.99
00701872	Beginner's – Level 1 Book/Audio & DVD	$19.95
00650743	Book/Audio/DVD with Ukulele	$39.99
00701002	Level 2 Book/Audio	$9.99
00702484	Level 2 Songbook Book/Audio	$12.99
00703290	Starter	$24.99

Play Viola Today!
00142679	Level 1 Book/Audio	$9.99

Play Violin Today!
00699748	Level 1 Book/Audio	$9.99
00701320	Level 2 Book/Audio	$9.99
00321076	DVD	$14.99
00701700	Songbook Book/Audio	$12.99
00701876	Beginner's – Level 1 Book/Audio & DVD	$19.95

HAL•LEONARD®

www.halleonard.com

The Drum Play-Along™ Series will help you play your favorite songs quickly and easily! Just follow the drum notation, listen to the audio to hear how the drums should sound, and then play-along using the separate backing tracks. The lyrics are also included for reference. The audio files are enhanced so you can adjust the recording to any tempo without changing pitch!

AUDIO ACCESS INCLUDED

1. Pop/Rock
00699742....................$14.99

2. Classic Rock
00699741....................$15.99

3. Hard Rock
00699743....................$15.99

4. Modern Rock
00699744....................$15.99

5. Funk
00699745....................$15.99

6. '90s Rock
00699746....................$17.99

7. Punk Rock
00699747....................$14.99

8. '80s Rock
00699832....................$15.99

9. Cover Band Hits
00211599....................$16.99

10. blink-182
00699834....................$16.99

11. Jimi Hendrix Experience: Smash Hits
00699835....................$17.99

12. The Police
00700268....................$16.99

13. Steely Dan
00700202....................$16.99

15. The Beatles
00256656....................$16.99

16. Blues
00700272....................$16.99

17. Nirvana
00700273....................$15.99

18. Motown
00700274....................$15.99

19. Rock Band: Modern Rock Edition
00700707....................$17.99

20. Rock Band: Classic Rock Edition
00700708....................$14.95

21. Weezer
00700959....................$14.99

22. Black Sabbath
00701190....................$16.99

23. The Who
00701191....................$16.99

24. Pink Floyd – Dark Side of the Moon
00701612....................$14.99

25. Bob Marley
00701703....................$17.99

26. Aerosmith
00701887....................$15.99

27. Modern Worship
00701921....................$16.99

28. Avenged Sevenfold
00702388....................$17.99

29. Queen
00702389....................$16.99

30. Dream Theater
00111942....................$24.99

31. Red Hot Chili Peppers
00702992....................$19.99

32. Songs for Beginners
00704204....................$14.99

33. James Brown
00117422....................$16.99

34. U2
00124470....................$16.99

35. Buddy Rich
00124640....................$19.99

36. Wipe Out & 7 Other Fun Songs
00125341....................$16.99

37. Slayer
00139861....................$17.99

38. Eagles
00143920....................$16.99

39. Kiss
00143937....................$16.99

40. Stevie Ray Vaughan
00146155....................$16.99

41. Rock Songs for Kids
00148113....................$14.99

42. Easy Rock Songs
00148143....................$14.99

45. Bon Jovi
00200891....................$16.99

46. Mötley Crüe
00200892....................$16.99

47. Metallica: 1983-1988
00234340....................$19.99

48. Metallica: 1991-2016
00234341....................$19.99

49. Top Rock Hits
00256655....................$16.99

51. Deep Purple
00278400....................$16.99

52. More Songs for Beginners
00278403....................$14.99

HAL•LEONARD®

Visit Hal Leonard Online at
www.halleonard.com

Prices, contents and availability subject to change without notice and may vary outside the US.

YOU CAN'T BEAT OUR DRUM BOOKS!